# Burnt Letters

CHRISTINA DITCHKOFSKY

For more information, email info@christinaditchkofsky.com

ISBN: 979-8-89694-400-3 - Ebook
ISBN: 979-8-89694-401-0 - Paperback
ISBN: 979-8-89694-541-3 - Hardcover

## DOWNLOAD FREE GIFT

# Free e-Book

If you're still asking, "Was it really that bad?"

Begin with:

→ "It Wasn't That Bad"

**BONUS**
**Back of Book**

Chapter-by-Chapter e-Book

# Dedication

To every rebellious little girl, every wild, radiant woman who's ever been told she was too loud, too emotional, too much—May it teach you never to shrink, to never chase love that hurts, and to never mistake silence for peace. Let this be the bolt cutter that breaks every chain we never asked to carry. May you live loud, bright, wild, and worthy. Always.

To my soul-sisters, Wendy and Annie, for being there through every heartbreak that turned into a lesson.

To the brother I never had, Dion — you showed up when it mattered most, with heart, humor, and loyalty.

To my therapists — those who truly heard me, guided me, and held up the mirror when I needed it most. And to that one therapist... yeah, you — the one who called me "fucking stupid." May your license be reviewed accordingly.

In memory of my grandmother, Audrey, who taught me patience, quiet strength, the sacred order of God, self, and responsibilities... and most of all, how to love with a complete and open heart.

To **every woman** in the *secret club*—the ones who've whispered in parking lots, bathrooms, inboxes, *"How do*

*I leave?"* This book is for you. I know that look in your eyes. I know the cost of freedom. I promise you're not crazy, and you're not alone.

To everyone who ever asked me, *"Why didn't you just leave?"*—I hope this book breaks your heart wide open. I hope it answers your question in a way I never could with words alone.

This book is not just mine. It belongs to every woman who was told to stay quiet, to behave, to endure.

It belongs to the ones still stuck, still scared, still trying to find a way out.

You are not too broken.

You are not too late.

You are not alone.

> — Keep shining bright, don't you dare
> shrink to the size of the room.

"Somewhere in this small world, you can find a place where everyone appreciates you more than you think you deserve."

M.F. Moonzajer

"The biggest mistake you can make is to believe that you are powerless in the face of narcissistic abuse. Remember, they are only powerful if you give them power."

Shahida Arabi

# Content Note

This book includes descriptions of emotional abuse, domestic violence, childhood trauma, sexual abuse, gaslighting, and family dysfunction. It also explores themes of codependency, generational trauma, complex post-traumatic stress, and survival responses.

Some material may be distressing or activating for readers with personal experience of trauma. Please consider reading at your own pace, pausing as needed, and seeking support if difficult emotions arise.

If you are currently experiencing abuse or are in crisis, professional and advocacy resources are available. This book is not a substitute for mental health treatment or professional care.

If you are in immediate danger, contact local emergency services. In the United States, the National Domestic Violence Hotline is available at 1-800-799-7233 or via thehotline.org.

You are not alone.

— Christina Ditchkofsky

For readers who want a structured way to process their experience, the free Chapter-by-Chapter Journal Prompts are available here:

https://subscribepage.io/Burnt-Letters-FreeGift

# Contents

> No one really knows why they are alive until
> they know what they'd die for.
> — Reverend Dr. Martin Luther King Jr.

# Prologue

*What was I willing to die for*— a question I never thought I'd have to answer. But there I was— pinned against the doorway, cold steel gouging deeper into my temple, my boyfriend's breath hot on my face.

"Chrissy, nobody cares about you," Frank said. "I could kill you right now, and you wouldn't even be missed."

My life flashed before my eyes—two failed marriages, buried trauma, broken pieces of a girl who had tried so hard to be loved.

And yet...I felt calm.

*Breathe, Chrissy, Breathe.*

I wasn't scared. Not of death. Not anymore.

Not being scared, that terrified me more than the gun.

I knew at that moment I had to get out. I could not keep living this way. But all I could think of was how did I get in this fucking mess anyway, and who would believe the bullshit I had been through?

In April 2014, my second husband moved out, and our divorce was finalized by August. I had added to my collection of failed romantic relationships. Yet this second divorce was markedly different from my first. This time, I started questioning whether anyone could genuinely love me. *Am I the problem?*

I stood in the wreckage of my life and asked myself the hardest question of all:

*Who the fuck am I?*

I had no answer. I'd lost myself somewhere between the roles I was told to play—wife, mother, fixer of boo-boos— and the wounds I was too afraid to face.

After my second divorce, I swore I'd stay single. At least until I figured myself out.

The echoes of the past haunted me.

"Chrissy, you are too hard on men," my first husband, Joseph, had said. "Your expectations are unrealistic."

I got my nose pierced. It felt like a rebellion. Or punishment. Or maybe both. A physical mark for failing at love.

It was like déjà vu with a different face. A few years later, I stood in my kitchen as my soon-to-be second ex-husband, Austin, said almost the exact same words: "Chrissy, you are very hard on the men in your life, and your expectations in a relationship are unrealistic."

Once my second marriage ended, I got a tattoo of a red poppy flower on my ring finger—my father's favorite flower. It symbolized death—another failed marriage.

I was only seventeen when I married for the first time—young, naïve, and pregnant. After the births of my second and third children, I was drowning in postpartum depression, isolated and invisible. There was no time for self-care. I had three kids and a husband who depended on me.

As the years passed, my anger grew. In the beginning, therapy didn't help because I couldn't reveal the root of my anger. I received a diagnosis of bipolar disorder and depression. The doctor prescribed lithium and Prozac. But numbing the pain didn't fix the damage—it just blurred the edges of reality.

Trust was an issue for me. I sabotaged every relationship I entered. My emotions were a daily rollercoaster—I never knew what mood I would be in from one day to the next. I had unrealistic expectations of love, trusted the wrong people, and gravitated toward emotionally unavailable men.

Yet this was the only life I knew, and it was how everyone in my immediate circle had come to expect me to behave.

After my second divorce, with a heart filled with grief, I started to see the pattern for the first time. *Toxic relationships weren't just a part of my life—they were my life.* I had been surviving chaos for so long, I didn't know what peace felt like.

Then, in my mid-forties, I finally found a therapist who didn't flinch at my truth. Who didn't try to fix me—just handed me a mirror. That's when I hear the words: Complex PTSD (C-PTSD). And for the first time, things started to make sense as I unpacked all my shit.

As I learned more about C-PTSD, I began to understand my past decisions better. I realized I could not return to my old life; I had to stop the emotional rollercoaster, confront my deepest fears, and rebuild a new life. This time, I had the insight to see why I felt so lost.

With my trusty journal and favorite pen in hand, I started changing my thoughts and rewriting my story—a story in which Chrissy wasn't a broken little girl.

She wasn't too much.

She wasn't unlovable.

She wasn't a mistake.

The instinct to retreat and hide after trauma is intense— to bury the truth, smooth it over, pretend we're fine. I tried that. For years, I was the faultless victim, the ideal liar—I wore shame like a second skin and called it protection.

But eventually, the truth catches up. It leaks into our relationships, our bodies, and our self-worth. And that moment—*that* moment in the bathroom with Frank — was my reckoning.

I realized that hiding wasn't working anymore.

Because when death knocked, I didn't flinch.

And that scared the hell out of me.

# Chapter 1

## Rose-Colored Glasses

I never felt like I belonged—not in my family, not in my relationships, not even in my own skin. I used to wonder if I was a gypsy or maybe an alien dropped on Earth by mistake. Maybe adopted. Anything that explained the gnawing feeling that I was the Black Sheep, born to stand out in a world that didn't want to understand me.

I wore rose-colored glasses for self-preservation. They weren't just for love—they filtered every part of my life. I wore them far longer than I should have, and by the time I finally took them off, the damage had already been done.

After my second divorce, I started journaling my thoughts and feelings in hopes of finding a spiritual awakening—some miracle, a quick fix to solve all my relationship problems.

Also after my second divorce, I signed up for graduate school to finally achieve my lifelong dream of becoming a psychiatric nurse practitioner. I was going to start school in January. This was going to be my year of putting Chrissy first!

I devoured book after book in hopes of healing my broken soul. I read Kerri Hummingbird Lawnby's *Awakening Me: One Woman's Journey to Self-Love* and Enitan O. Bereola II's Gentle *Woman: Etiquette for a Lady, From a Gentleman.* I then read Don Miguel Ruiz's books. I started with *The Four Agreements* and then moved on to *The Mastery of Love.*

But, as I read each new book, I realized that I needed to learn boundaries—no, I needed to learn how to uphold healthy boundaries.

I'm not sure if it was loneliness or the challenge of reaching for my dreams, but I remember feeling so afraid.

One night, in desperation, with red and swollen eyes and a throbbing head, I gathered incense and candles. The full moon's light guided me as I placed stones and crystals in a circle around me. I lit the candles, and the dragon's blood incense burned like a warning. Sobbing on the living room floor, I called out to something— God, the universe, my higher self, anything that might listen, "I don't care what you do – fix me. Please... bring anything you want into my life to fully break me wide open...I cannot live this way anymore—I'm so broken."

I wrote letters I knew I'd never send. One to my father, asking forgiveness for the heartaches I put him through, two more to my ex-husbands—raw, unfinished goodbyes laced with guilt and sorrow. I set the letters on fire. Watched them curl and disappear like the versions of me that had lived for others too long.

And that's when the universe answered.

The next day, I woke up, took a deep breath, and thought, *Okay, today is the day things are going to change for me.*

I leaped out of bed and laughed as my dog Daizy wiggled her way out from under the covers. I said, "Daizy, let's go; time to tackle this day!" I have been an early riser for as long as I can remember. Maybe my grandmother instilled this trait in me. Even before the *5-Second Rule* was written, as soon as my alarm went off, I would jump straight out of bed and get moving.

My oldest daughter, Lynne, once said to me, "Mom, you're the type of person that when your feet hit the floor the Devil says, 'Oh, shit, she's up.'"

I planned to meet Lee, an acquaintance I had met through my friend Dave. Dave lived in the same development as me. He was a bit older than I was, but a great friend. He encouraged me to pursue my graduate degree, and occasionally, we went out for breakfast.

Lee was married, and I would meet him at a diner down the road from time to time. I was researching why married men cheat on their wives and think it's okay, and Lee was more than happy to be seen in public with me and answer all my questions. Lee had been married for over thirty years to the same woman and was known for being flirty with younger women. I once asked him *Why do you meet with me in public places? I mean, aren't you afraid your wife will find out?*

Lee said, "No, and I don't care, really. There are things she doesn't give me anymore. Maybe...if she saw me with another woman, she would act better towards me."

After we finished our lunch, we waited to pay; this guy sat at the counter and asked Lee if I was his sister.

Lee said, "Frank, you know my sister."

"Is that your girlfriend?"

"No!"

The guy turned to me. "Hey, if you're not his girlfriend, can I get your number?"

I asked the waitress for a pen, grabbed his greasy napkin, scribbled my number, and dropped it on his half-eaten plate. "God help me," I muttered as I walked out.

Lee looked horrified. "You shouldn't have done that."

"He's not gonna call." I shrugged.

*What kind of man would call a woman after she just insulted him and acted like that?*

But he did.

I'm unsure if it was a curse, stupidity, or what, but I had this uncanny ability to leap before I thought. Usually, I jumped with both feet straight in, and then, while I sank in the quicksand, I'd think, *Hmm, maybe I shouldn't have done that.*

The next day, the guy from the diner called and wanted to meet for lunch.

What did I have to lose? I had the day off from work, and it was supposed to be a beautiful December day with unusually warm temperatures in the mid-60s.

Frank and I met at an Indian restaurant. When I pulled into the parking lot, he was in a small red sports car. It was old, but it didn't have any rust on it. I thought he wasn't my type when he stepped out of the car. He was shorter than most of the men I usually dated and dressed in jeans and a wrinkled T-shirt. I am five feet seven inches tall and like to wear three-inch heels, so I try to date men at least six feet tall. He had this small brown leather pouch tied around his neck by a brown string.

As I approached him, the aroma of earthy tones mixed with the scent of musk hit my nose. It was not a cologne I had ever smelled before. I asked him, "What kind of cologne is that?"

Frank said, "Patchouli. It is an essential oil."

I was obsessed with essential oils—the first flicker of deeper curiosity was lit, one that would eventually set my soul on fire.

He thanked me for meeting him and walked me into the restaurant. It was set up like a buffet. We entered a large room with tables and trays of different types of Indian food. I had never had Indian food before, so I had no idea what to try.

I grabbed a little from each of the trays.

We walked down a few steps to a sunroom with tables in front of the windows. The sun's warmth felt good. The view was amazing. I could see the interstate and the pine trees lining the highway.

Growing up, I passed by this place every day, but I had never been here before.

Frank and I sat down, and at first, we made small talk.

He asked me what I did for fun, my hobbies, my favorite foods, and what type of man I was interested in.

I told him, "I love hiking outdoors or working in my flowerbeds and vegetable gardens. I haven't gone to too many restaurants, but I love Italian food. As for a man, I really don't have a type per se; I'm not looking for a relationship. I just would like someone to do things with from time to time."

Frank gestured to the waitress to fill our glasses with water.

Frank went into detail about traveling to New Zealand, Costa Rica, and the band he played in.

Frank was nothing like any of the men I had ever dated. I always seemed to date uneducated men or businessmen who tried too hard to impress me. Frank was down-to-earth yet knowledgeable and didn't seem to care if I liked him or not. He just asked questions about me for the most part.

He made me feel comfortable, at ease, like a warm blanket on a cold night.

I was shocked when he said he was just a few years ahead of me in school and I wondered why we had never met before today. I could not believe we had gone to the same school, lived in the same neighborhood, and had never bumped into each other before yesterday.

After we ate and chatted, he asked me if I wanted to go on a hike on top of Big Pocono. I immediately said, "Yes." I love to hike and be outside. It was such a beautiful, warm day.

We walked to the cash register, and I said, "I will pay for my own meal." I was a strong, independent woman. In my first marriage, I did not hold down a full-time job. I put my dreams on hold for my family. Now I had money.

Besides, I didn't know this guy and didn't want him to think I was looking for someone to sponge off.

He gestured for me to go ahead of him and pay for my meal, and then he opened the brown leather bag around his neck and pulled out some cash.

When we got outside, Frank offered to drive us to the top of the mountain just a few miles away, and then he would bring me back to my car.

I agreed—naïvely and eagerly. I jumped in his car.

There was something about him I couldn't place. The patchouli, the way he didn't try too hard, the pouch around his neck. It wasn't attraction—it was curiosity... maybe fate. Or perhaps the universe is testing whether I meant it when I asked to be broken wide open.

Growing up, I could see the mountain from my house, and my family even watched the fireworks light up on the 4th of July. Yet I had never been on any of the trails on top of Big Pocono.

As Frank and I drove up the windy road to the top of the mountain. I texted my friend Liz to let her know where I was going.

I looked over at him and said, "You're not taking me up here to kill me, are you?"

He laughed and said, "How do I know you're not going to kill *me*?"

I followed Frank up that mountain, thinking maybe I was saying yes to a hike. But deep down, I was saying yes to something else. Something I didn't fully understand yet.

I didn't know it then, but that day changed everything.

When all you know is fight or
flight, red flags and butterflies all
feel the same. — Cindy Cherie

# Chapter 2

## Setting The Trap

It didn't start with red flags. It started with butterflies.

December swept me into a dizzying blur of warmth, attention, and connection—everything I thought I'd been waiting for. After just one date, Frank invited me to his place. It turned out he lived only a few miles from me, which felt like fate. *How have I never seen him before?*

He was charming and ambitious. He was the kind of man who cooked Thai food like a pro and talked philosophy over tea. I remember thinking, *He's perfect*.

But that's the thing about traps—they're always baited with what you crave most.

Frank was an entrepreneur. He owned his own rental business and had multiple apartments. I was a nurse, so this was perfect for us to spend ample time getting to know each other.

A few weeks into our relationship, he cooked me drunken noodles. It was the first time I had ever had Thai food. I remember watching him as he whisked up the meal with ease.

After dinner, he asked me if I liked tea.

"Oh yes, I drink tea with my grandmother all the time."

Frank's kitchen had the original cupboards, a pantry built into the wall near the table, and an island that extended out, separating the kitchen from the dining room. The island had short upper cabinets with sliding glass doors that opened on both sides. Frank slid open the doors on the dining room side and pulled out a few herbal teas.

I said, "I'll have the Orange Zest."

We made our tea and wandered into the living room. The living room was toasty from the woodstove, and we snuggled up on the couch. We talked about when he was a professor at a local university.

"I quit because education is filled with politics, rules, and regulations that have nothing to do with teaching the students. All the education system wants to do is push people through. Give them their degree no matter how dumb they are. I just couldn't buy into that system."

He told me that after his mom died, his dad got sick, and he had to move back home to take care of him. He asked about my family, and we discovered that my grandmother and his mom had been friends.

Even though I had failed to keep out of a relationship, I told myself I would stay firm with my boundaries. I shared with Frank how I would not sleep with him until we were together for a while, and he was tested for STDs.

Frank agreed. He said, "I will, but I don't have health insurance. Society doesn't make it easy for entrepreneurs to obtain such benefits. But I'll look into it."

It sounded reasonable, but part of me wondered if this was just a way to sidestep the boundary I had clearly set.

One cold afternoon, we drank wine, and one thing led to another, and before I knew what had happened, we made love.

It felt right.

The next day, I felt like I'd betrayed myself.

Nothing was said, and we continued to get to know each other.

One thing I learned about Frank was that he was extremely curious about my life. Frank asked me about my dreams, and I told him I was starting school in January to fulfill my goal of becoming a nurse practitioner.

Frank immediately sat up straight, looked at me, and stated, "I don't think I could seriously date someone going to school. It will definitely get in the way of building a strong foundation for our relationship.

Without a strong foundation, a relationship is built on shifting sand."

It was the first time I felt the ground beneath us shift. But instead of standing firm, I crumbled.

I dropped out of school.

When Dave found out I dropped out of school he said, "This is your dream! Please don't give up on your dreams for some guy you just met!"

But I ignored his advice.

I told myself it was my choice, but the truth was I wanted his approval more than I wanted my own future.

The next day kicked off my stretch of three scheduled shifts.

I loved the unpredictability of work—you never knew what you were walking into. No two days were ever the same. One moment, I might be monitoring a patient fresh out of the Cath Lab, checking vital signs every fifteen minutes, and scanning for signs of internal bleeding. The next moment, I'd sprint down the hall to a Code Blue.

I lived for that rush—the constant interaction, the ever-shifting pace, the electric edge of knowing that life and death could flip in a second.

Frank invited me over for the night on my last day of work.

Snow covered the ground, but the sun was starting to melt away the remnants of winter. That night, as we watched *Harold and Maude*, an old 1970s romance, Frank asked me if I wanted to go on an adventure the next day, hiking in the snow.

We woke up early. As I sat at the kitchen table drinking my coffee, Frank made us breakfast. I watched in amazement as he prepared a meal. I had never been with a man who cooked more than a hot dog or fried eggs. I watched Frank dice red potatoes, sweet potatoes, mushrooms, and onions, and then whipped up a vegetable omelet and whole-wheat toast.

After breakfast, we set off on our adventure.

Frank and I wandered around the woods, exploring. We came across a few old stone buildings, one of which had a shallow well built into the floor, complete with a hand pump to access the water.

We walked a bit further and found a stone footbridge that led across a stream. The air was cold, and the water had frozen over. The frozen water curled over the edges of the banks and made a ribbon of ice running down the stream. I found a shallow area where I could stand and take pictures of the ice formations. I discovered a rock that, when you looked at it just right, seemed to have two eyes, a nose, and a mouth. I said, "Frank, look. A human face."

I loved to explore and look at things most people miss. I lay in the snow near the bridge, taking pictures; I said, "I know fairies live under this bridge. Look at how the sticks are laid up like a little house, with the moss covering the top as a roof.

Frank agreed, "Don't you just look so cute and innocent lying there exploring your surroundings. Jump up on the railing and I'll take your picture."

My feet were soggy, and my toes were numb. I said, "I think we need to head back to the house to warm up."

"Sounds good. Let's get some grub."

After lunch, Frank introduced me to his two best friends, Tom and Bill. Tom had been his friend for a long time, and Bill was a young man Frank was mentoring in the entrepreneurial business. Frank taught Bill how to buy apartment buildings, rehab them, and understand the legal aspects of owning his own business.

As our relationship grew, I found myself starting to cancel plans with family and friends to spend more time with him. And if I had plans he knew about, he would call me suddenly to tell me he had planned this exciting hike or wanted me to meet his friend. I was so addicted to him that I would cancel plans with the other person to see him. It was scary how fast our relationship was going.

Every time I was around Frank, I savored the compliments like fine wine. He would tell me how amazing I was and that I was perfect for him, and he couldn't believe it had taken this long to meet me.

I felt intoxicated with him.

He cooked for me and took me on hikes. Frank often told me how unique I was and how lucky he felt to have my attention. He said he knew I could have any man I wanted, but I chose him.

He planned a vacation to Costa Rica.

I couldn't tell if we were building something real or if it was just a carefully crafted distraction to keep me chasing the illusion.

We spent hours together lying on his sofa, learning everything we could about each other's interests and desires. I felt like I was the focal point of his universe.

One evening, I said, "I think I'm falling in love with you."

Frank shook his head, reached for the TV remote, clicked it off, and turned towards me. "Go and love some more."

"What...what does that mean?"

"It's from *Maude and Harold*. Ya, know what, it is probably my fault you fell in love with me so fast. Maybe we should slow this down and not see each other so much."

"I'm sorry for telling you I love you. It felt natural to me."

"Chrissy, it's unnatural. I specifically told you that we needed to build our relationship on solid ground. This is not solid ground. This is still sand, and we are shifting."

He jumped up and said, "You wanna grab some pizza? I'm hungry."

I was embarrassed and wanted to talk about our relationship, but I could see Frank was uncomfortable and didn't want to talk anymore, so I said, "Yes, I love pizza."

Frank took me down the road to a pizza place. As we paid the owner and walked out, Frank said, "I used to date her, but all she did was boast about her money."

*That was odd. Of all the places around here where we could get pizza, why would he take me to a place where he dated someone?*

We had been seeing each other for about five weeks when he voiced his concerns, telling me, "I don't have the energy to work on such a new relationship. I thought by now we would have a firmer foundation, but the sand is unsteady, and the walls are shifting."

My heart dropped to the floor, the hair on my arms stood straight up, and it hurt to breathe. I froze, didn't know what to say.

Honestly, I didn't know what to do. I looked at Frank, but he didn't say anything. I think I was looking for some reassurance that we were okay. That maybe he was not seriously breaking up with me.

But he just stared at me.

I turned around and walked towards the back door.

I reached for the doorknob and paused for a moment. I wanted him to stop me, to fight for me. But the silence said more than any words ever *could*.

As I drove home, I started to question myself: *Did I rush this relationship? Was I so afraid of losing yet another love that I am holding on too tightly? Am I the problem in all my relationships?*

I was supposed to work the next day, but I called out. I was emotionally in no condition to leave the house. Frank had put a spell on me, and I felt lost without him. I called him two times, but he did not answer.

I sat down and typed out an email.

> I'm unsure if I should keep reaching out to you. But I walked out your door, so I know you won't come looking for me. Maybe that's pride. Maybe it's just pain.
>
> I love you, and I miss you. And in time, I will understand this. My biggest regret is not finding the words you could hear to tell you how safe I felt in your arms and how deeply I believed in us.
>
> You said I sounded angry, but it wasn't anger. It was fear, passion, and desperation not to be abandoned again.
>
> I have now reached out to you twice. I will not beg, but I will reach out, as I did. It is what I needed from you—to meet me halfway, just a few times.
>
> I wish you the best, no matter what you decide or do not decide with us. And I thank you for showing me love. My heart will never be the same again—it is fully alive.

His reply evoked a range of emotions from anger to hurt to confusion.

> I really do not want to talk to you...

as for your belongings...you abandoned them...

I am not of the opinion that these "things" are my responsibility...

Nonetheless, you may pick them up next week on Monday or whatever day you have off—

You understand me now?

I do not see it that way...

The thing you called anger was confusion...I do not understand you... Nor do I have the energy to work so hard on such a new relationship. It needed to flow naturally...and it didn't...other than the kisses and sex...which, by the way, were wonderful and did feel natural...

I made it very clear that direct communication was imperative. You either lacked that ability, maturity, or both.

I am not a "NEW AGE BELIEVER," I believe very much in being a discerning person. I choose very carefully the people I hold dear and close to my heart. Unfortunately, I don't have room for another friend...unless they have something to offer me other than drama and chaos...

I am not interested in being your friend, other than these words...

I don't have much for you anymore.

See you next week!

Why did I even email him? Why was I still begging for clarity from a man who had already shut the door?

I barely knew him. And yet he cracked something open in me. A wound I didn't realize still needed tending.

Caring for someone can be beautiful. But love that requires you to shrink yourself to be chosen—that's not love. That's a warning.

I mistook attention for affection. I confused intensity for intimacy. And somewhere deep down, I already knew—

This was never just about Frank.

It was about the little girl inside me still searching for safety in unsafe places.

# Chapter 3

## Leaving a Trail of Breadcrumbs

I cried for days.

I was desperate for closure, though now I know it was never closure I was seeking—it was another hit of hope.

I went to work and confided in a colleague of mine, Shawn. He was the director of the critical care units at the hospital where I worked, and he and I connected. I felt like I could trust him; he was older and very professional. He gave great advice, and we shared a lot of the same values and interests—writing, for one. I often sat in his office, pouring my heart out about one problem or another.

"There must be something wrong with him for writing you such a nasty email. Besides, he wouldn't even support your goal of getting your nurse practitioner degree."

Shawn said, "Why are you crying?"

"Because he's gone," I whispered.

"No," he said. "You're crying because you gave your heart to someone who never intended to hold it with care. That's not love, that's loss masquerading as hope."

Shawn told me it was best to leave him alone: "He's no good for you."

But I could not be alone. I was so empty inside without a man. I lacked boundaries, and I kept calling Frank. He never answered, so I left several messages, begging to see him one more time and retrieve the things I had left at his place. I didn't care about my things; I just knew if he let me see him one more time, he would want me back.

My desperate cry for help was heard and he called me back.

He told me I could come over and grab my things off his back porch before he put them in the trash.

As I drove to Frank's house, I wondered if he would *let me in*.

I knocked and stared at the doorknob, silently praying, *Please open the door...please open the door....Please just let me see you one more time.*

I heard footsteps approaching, and the backdoor knob twisted open. There were the familiar brown boots I was praying to see.

"There are your things. Take them and leave."

"Frank, please let me come in and have a cup of tea with you one last time."

Frank smiled, stepped to the side, and motioned for me to come in.

What I didn't realize then was that he was never planning to love me—he was only keeping me just close enough, breadcrumb by breadcrumb, so I wouldn't notice how lost I'd become in the woods.

After our first breakup, things were as they had begun in the first few months: romantic and smooth sailing—at least through my rose-colored glasses, everything was perfect.

The illusion of Frank was about to be stained. One day, I woke up to a message on Facebook from Frank's ex-girlfriend Stacy.

Stacy wrote that Frank was still talking to her and telling her he loves her.

I didn't know what to do. I was working with my friend and showed it to her. We both agreed that Stacy was just jealous and obviously didn't want to break up with him.

But then Stacy sent me screenshots of emails between her and Frank. Frank said in one of the emails, "This new chick is crazy and driving me nuts. I miss you."

Later that evening, I called Frank to talk about it with him. He told me to come over, and we could talk about it.

"Our relationship is new; I was with Stacy for over three and a half years. I do miss her at times, and I do care about her still, but that is where it ends with her. I know she and I have no future together."

I asked him about the screenshot of me "driving him nuts."

Frank laughed and said, "You do drive me nuts, but not in a bad way."

He grabbed me and said, "Don't let Stacy upset you. She is just jealous that I'm so happy with someone besides her."

I let the conversation end, but Stacy continued to message me for weeks about her and Frank's conversations.

I tried putting my efforts into more positive places, like having Frank meet some of my friends.

One evening, I sat in a cozy restaurant with Frank and one of my closest friends from work, Kelly, for a dinner we had planned weeks ago. The surroundings were energetic, filled with laughter and chatter, and they were excited to finally meet. However, the evening took an unexpected turn.

As we settled into our meals, Kelly asked a question that interested me. Curious about the answer, I instinctively reached for my phone lying on the table to look it up. As my fingers brushed against the screen, Frank snatched my phone away, his expression a mix of authority and disdain. "We do not use phones at the table."

The air in the restaurant shifted the moment he snatched my phone. Laughter at nearby tables kept echoing, but inside, everything stilled. My cheeks burned. I laughed it off, like I had learned to do in childhood—when embarrassment or shame felt too big to hold.

Noticing the tension, my friend kicked me under the table, signaling me discreetly. "I need to go to the bathroom, and I need you to come with me," she whispered urgently.

I nodded, sensing something was off, but I followed her eagerly, hoping to escape the bizarre interaction for a moment.

Once we reached the restroom, Kelly spun around to face me, her eyes wide with concern. "What are you doing?"

"What do you mean?"

"Get away from him, he's crazy."

I couldn't help but laugh, as if dismissing her remark would make everything okay. "Why?" I questioned, genuinely perplexed.

She shook her head and said, "Because you let him take your phone?"

The gravity of Kelly's words began to settle in, but I tried to rationalize his behavior and said, "Well, everyone has healthy boundaries, and that one is his. I think I can respect him and not be on my phone."

She stared at me for a moment. Then she reached for the door and turned towards me.

"One day, you're going to look back and hate yourself for not leaving now," she said. "Don't let it get that far," and then she left me standing there with a growing sense of unease.

That moment with Kelly should have been my wake-up call, but I brushed it off—just like I had brushed off so many red flags before. Still, something about the way she walked away stayed with me.

*"Until you heal the wounds of your past, you are going to bleed. You can bandage the bleeding with food, with alcohol, with drugs, with work, with cigarettes, with sex, but eventually, it will all ooze through and stain your life. You must find the strength to open the wounds, stick your hands inside and pull out the core of the pain that is holding you in your past, the memories and then make peace with them"* — Author unknown.

I told Frank, Kelly and I planned a trip Jamaica.

"You planned a trip without me?"

I reminded him about our trip to Puerto Rico, eager to appease him.

"When?" he asked.

"March."

"That's when I was going to take you to Puerto Rico," he snapped.

I never asked if he had booked anything—I didn't want to ruin the illusion.

The next day, I told Kelly I wasn't going. She just looked at me. "You mean you can't do both? He can't work around it?"

"He didn't say when we're going," I mumbled.

She rolled her eyes and walked away.

My boss approved my two-week vacation, and we started planning the trip.

But every time I tried to talk about purchasing our flight tickets and booking the hotel he would say, "Tomorrow I'll look into it."

A few weeks later, Frank said he was too busy to travel.

And just like that, I had lost the trip—and hurt a friend.

I told myself it was fine. That maybe next time would be different.

That vacation was more than a missed trip. It was a mirror. A moment that revealed just how much of myself I had abandoned in the name of love.

> Evil rarely looks evil until it accomplishes its goal; it gains entrance by appearing attractive, desirable, and perfectly legitimate. It is a baited and camouflaged trap. — Kyle Snodgrass

# Chapter 4

## Prepping For The Main Course

I thought it was love. Now, I know it was a test. A trap dressed as a dream.

"Hey, why don't you stay with me for those two weeks? This way, we can get to know each other more closely and see if we're compatible to live together."

That was it. The invitation I'd been waiting for. The pain of the canceled Puerto Rico trip vanished. So did the sting of canceling Jamaica. I was about to play house with Frank—for real.

Before I met Frank, I had planned a trip to Florida to visit my son, Jack, with my oldest daughter, Lynne.

As Frank and I were chatting one evening, I mentioned that I was going to Florida for a few days with my daughter in a week.

He didn't say much. Just got quiet.

The silence said more than words ever could.

A day later, he asked, "Are you punishing me for canceling Puerto Rico?"

"No... I planned this before I even met you. I miss my son."

He seemed to accept my explanation.

But, when I was gone, he called me every few hours. Texted nonstop.

Lynne looked at me and said, "Mom, what is wrong with him?"

Jack just said, "Ignore him."

I told them, "He's just worried about me."

What I didn't say was... it felt good to be needed.

I hadn't realized I was mistaking control for concern.

When I got home, Frank had a welcome-back dinner prepared for me. He apologized for calling me so much but said he was worried I would dump him like his girlfriend in college did.

He told me how he and she had planned to move to New Zealand together, but when the day came to leave, he showed up with his suitcases, and she laughed at him and said, "You're not going with me. I bought one ticket, and it's for me only."

Listening to him open up about his hurt, I thought he was protecting our relationship.

I went to visit my lifelong best friend, Beth, for lunch. We had been friends since elementary school, and always kept our friendship alive, no matter what happened. I had told her about Frank and his idea of moving in with him. She said, "Go for it. It's just a trial. You only live once."

March came around so fast. I packed up my things, and Daizy and I both went over to Frank's house for two weeks.

We talked about planting a garden together and planting seeds in his greenhouse in the attic.

He lived in an old house he inherited after his dad died. Frank converted it into a duplex, but no one lived on the other side at that time because Frank was in the middle of rehabbing it.

Frank's side of the house had a set of stairs that went up into the attic. It was a full-size attic with a partitioned-off room that Frank had insulated and heated for growing plants. We planted bell peppers, heirloom tomatoes, grape tomatoes, Italian plum tomatoes, broccoli, cauliflower, and jalapeno peppers.

I grew up on a farm and remember always having a huge vegetable garden. When I was little, my grandmother had a greenhouse behind her house where she grew her own plants and even sold them to the local community. I would spend hours watching her blend soil, peat moss, and vermiculite. She took her finger, poked a hole in the middle of the plastic seed starter packs, and dropped in a seed. Then, she would mist the soil gently. Every day, I walked from my house, crossed over the dirt path to my grandmother's driveway, and followed the narrow grassy path to the greenhouse to see if today the day was the seeds came to life.

I felt right at home preparing for the day Frank and I would harvest the fruits of our labor.

As Frank and I worked on planting the seeds, I said, "My grammy taught me how to can and make homemade spaghetti sauce and pickles. We can also make salsa if we get a lot of tomatoes."

"I like that idea. I can't wait," Frank said. "I also have strawberries in the garden, and we can make jam with them. Ya' know what, Chrissy, you are a very unique woman. Not many women know the old-fashioned ways. I really am glad I ran into you at the diner that day."

I was swallowing poison—one sugar-coated compliment at a time.

Frank showed me his studio in the backyard and told me about the band he used to play in.

He told me he had over a hundred guns hidden in the ceiling rafters.

"The government's trying to take our freedom," he said. "I have to be ready to protect myself."

I laughed it off at the time, thinking he was exaggerating—maybe even joking. But something in his eyes said otherwise. Still, I brushed it aside, told myself not to overthink it.

*Just another one of his quirks... right?*

The studio was a large open room with brightly colored framed four-foot by five-foot pieces of carpet hanging on the walls. A groovy lava lamp sat on a table in the corner, a disco ball hung from the ceiling rafters, and oriental rugs covered the floor. In the back corner was a drum set, and three microphone stands were placed in a circle with a camera on a tripod in the front of the room.

Frank walked over to one of the tables, lit some incense sticks, and placed them around the room. He told me that a few of his friends were working to form a new band and asked me if I wanted to hear one of the songs he was working on.

"Yes! I'd love that."

Frank knelt down, flipped on the amplifier, and ran his fingers over the strings, coaxing out a few notes as he tuned. Then, without a word, he began to play—and sing—just for me.

I asked him about his band. He said, "This is a new band I'm forming."

"Oh, what happened with your original band?"

"It's a long story, but the guys in the band didn't agree with my vision of where things were going. Honestly, it pissed me off. I mean, I built this studio, bought all the equipment, and even paid to record the CD. Oh, yeah, here." He handed me his CD.

"Wow, I can't wait to listen to it."

I nodded, but something about the way he said "I did it all" stuck with me.

At the time, I thought it meant he was driven.

We snuggled on the couch during the cold days, drank wine, and discussed future dreams.

I enjoyed going to the grocery store together to plan meals for the week and even planned a date night at his favorite Tai restaurant.

I love Kombucha and bought it at the store every week. I told Frank, "It's crazy how expensive this drink is."

He said, "We can make our own. It's easy."

"Really, let's do it. I hate spending all this money on this little bottle."

Frank looked online for the glass flip-top bottles and dug out a two-gallon glass jar from under the sink. We bought loose-leaf green and black tea for the base. To make Kombucha, we first had to develop a Scoby, a culture of bacteria and yeast created through the fermentation of tea and sugar.

We boiled the water, added the tea leaves, and let the tea steep until cool. Next, we strained out the loose tea, stirred in the sugar, and blended a handful of fresh strawberries. We added everything to the glass jar and waited for the Scoby to form.

One of my favorite days was spent with him, cutting firewood, loading it into his truck, and piling it on the porch.

I grew up with a wood stove in our basement; my dad had a woodshed out back. My first husband and I heated our entire house with the heat of our wood stove. We spend most of our summers cutting trees down on my family's property, splitting the wood, and stacking it in our woodshed.

"We really are quite compatible," he said. "Why don't you move in? You could save money... live here for free. Help me out."

The offer sounded practical. Generous. Perfect. But something in me paused, just for a second. Then I shook it off.

In my first marriage, I raised my three kids, kept the house clean, worked in the gardens, and tended to our chickens.

When that marriage ended, I went back to school and became a nurse. I had to walk away from my first house and did not have a vegetable garden or flower beds in my new home. I missed being home and working around the house, tending to the garden, cooking, and sewing.

If I moved in with Frank, I could save money, work less, and have more time for what I enjoyed. I told myself, "This is what love looks like." But part of me felt like I was auditioning. Like I had to earn my place. Prove my worth.

And I was damn good at making things beautiful— gardens, homes, dreams.

I called Beth. "He's perfect!" I told her about our plans.

"Just keep your house," she said.

"Of course," I replied.

"Well, girl, go for it. What could go wrong?"

"Oh, Beth, I keep waiting to wake up from this dream."

We laughed, and it was decided. I was moving in.

Frank's friend Tom stopped by the next day, and Frank filled him in on the good news.

"Whatever you do, don't sell your house," Tom said.

I laughed, awkwardly. "I'm not. I'm renting it."

He looked me dead in the eye.

"Good. Because when Frank's done with you, he'll kick you out."

I blinked. "What?"

"I'm just saying."

Frank laughed it off and changed the subject.

I told myself Tom was just bitter.

But that sentence would echo in my mind months later—louder than ever.

It was finalized, and the next day, we started packing my things and moving me in with Frank.

Frank helped me paint my house and write up a lease. A fellow nurse was looking for a place to stay, so we agreed on a monthly fee, and she signed a one-year lease.

Everything was working perfectly, and just in time, because the Scoby had formed on top of the tea mixture; time to make Kombucha.

After I moved in, Frank's old girlfriend Stacy messaged me to say she had heard I had moved in.

Of course she did.

Stacy wrote to me, "Don't you have any friends? What friend would let you move in with a guy you have only known for three months?"

I told Frank about the message, and he said, "I told Stacy you were moving in and that she needed to stop calling and emailing me." He said he told her he needed to concentrate on his new relationship and it was unfair to his new girlfriend to keep talking to her.

When I was a teenager, I pushed every boundary I could to the limit. I broke all the rules I could. I hated adults and just wanted to live my life on my own terms. Looking back, I know now that having boundaries was healthy and would have saved me from a lot of heartache.

I didn't know he was still talking to Stacy, but how gentlemanly he was to think of me and tell her to leave him alone out of respect for me.

I thought I was starting a new life.

Really, I was being invited into his.

But the door I stepped through wasn't a home—it was a setup.

I just didn't know it yet.

> Toxic people attach themselves like cinder blocks
> tied to your ankles, and then invite you for a swim
> in their poisoned waters. — John Mark Green

# Chapter 5

## Fluffing The Pillows

Moving in with Frank felt like stepping into a dream stitched together from vintage linens and sunbeams.

Frank's place was a two-story house with three bedrooms upstairs. He gave me the middle room to use as my office. As I was cleaning out the room, I found that it was filled with women's clothes, dog toys, and makeup. I asked Frank about these things.

He said, "Oh, they're Stacy's things. Sometimes she stayed here, and I guess she left some things in the closet."

I asked, "Doesn't she want them back?"

"I don't care if she does. She left them. You can throw them out."

A tight knot formed in my stomach as I shoved the bag into the trash. I didn't ask any more questions. I told myself I was claiming space—but part of me knew I was erasing a woman I'd never met.

I unpacked my college paintings and sewing supplies and envisioned my desk next to the double window, which overlooked the side yard and parts of the vegetable garden. The morning sunlight shone in brightly and was perfect for my plants.

I enjoyed sewing. My grandmother and mom taught me how to sew when I was younger. I used to make American Girl doll and Barbie clothes for my girls and applique pillows. I even made a quilt for the American Girl doll.

I moved all my plants to Frank's house, placed a few in my office, and put the rest in our room. Frank had been using the back bedroom, and we decided to clean out the front room, it was brighter and much larger.

We rented a floor sander from the local hardware store, and I refinished the hardwood floors. My dad was a jack-of-all-trades. He could do anything that needed to be built or repaired. I learned a lot from him. When I was growing up, my family had an array of tradesmen, and I don't think we ever paid anyone to fix things that broke. We just picked up the phone and called an uncle or cousin and traded services or offered them a favor in the future.

Frank reminded me a lot of my dad. He did all of his handiwork for his apartments.

Frank and I played house. We picked out olive green paint for the walls and transformed the front room into our dreamy little slice of heaven. We moved my queen-sized bed and golden yellow antique dressers into the new space.

He didn't like my bamboo headboard. He said, "I'll make us a new one with shelves for your books. I'll start tomorrow."

But my queen-sized bed was bigger than his, so we used it.

When I told him the story about my dressers, he said we could put them in the bedroom. Besides, the olive-green paint matched the leaves on the flowers perfectly!

My dresser came from upstate New York. I had been looking for the perfect vintage look for my bedroom to match my antique white bamboo headboard. I found exactly what I was looking for on eBay—one tall dresser with five drawers and a long dresser with a matching mirror attached to the top. The dressers were golden yellow, with dainty faded pansies hand-painted on the fronts of each drawer. The tall dresser had the flowers painted on the fronts of drawers to form a large flower bouquet in a vase. The paint was worn from time and chipped off in places. They were perfect!

Frank didn't have room for my antique claw-foot sofa, so we stored it in the loft of the garage.

I put my antique desk and chair, as well as the hutch that my ex-mother-in-law had given me, in my new office. I used the hutch to store my books. I did my best to read at least 100 books a year. I had boxes of books and my antique creamer collection sitting in the corner of the room. I picked up the pheasant shot by my dad and preserved by his friend who owned a taxidermy shop. *Hmmm, I think I'll hang it over my desk.* It was the only thing I got when my dad died.

Vintage items have always had a strong pull on my heart, and I'm not sure why. A friend told me I'm an old soul who has returned to earth several times.

Maybe it was because my grandmother, my dad's mother, had the most significant influence on my life.

My paternal grandmother was my safety net growing up. My parents fought a lot. I felt ignored and lost in chaos at home. My dad had an elaborate workshop set up in our basement, which he called his den, where he spent most of his life tinkering with one project after another. My mom was either busy cooking in the kitchen or lying on the living room sofa, lost in one of her smutty romance novels.

I spent most of my childhood two houses down the road at my grandmother's. My grandmother was the wisest, gentlest, kindest, and most loved woman I have ever met. She was *my everything*, my escape from the chaos of my family life, and the one I turned to at 17 when I found out I was pregnant. She taught me how to sew, grow vegetables, can and freeze my harvest, and make braided rugs. I was loved just as I was by her.

Frank gave me the old-time feeling of comfort that I had growing up on my grandmother's farm.

Frank and I planned meals together, went on date nights, sat on the couch watching *Penny Dreadful*, drank wine, and ate Ben & Jerry's ice cream.

I could finally be at ease because I was home.

Frank told me about his former wedding photography business and showed me all his old equipment.

I asked, "Can you teach me how to use one of those fancy cameras?"

He smiled and said, "Of course, baby."

He agreed to give me lessons over the next few weeks. He said, "I'll break down the lessons into small sessions where you will learn about using the various lenses, macro and micro. We will start your lessons tomorrow."

The weather was warming up, and we began working in the garden. I told Frank I had always wanted a greenhouse. I showed him a picture of a greenhouse that was made out of old windows. I told him I bought a few antique windows in hopes of building a greenhouse box one day.

I headed into work the next day. It was hectic, but I didn't mind—I genuinely loved spending time with my patients and their families.

Later in the shift, Shawn called me into his office.

"I just had a family member come by to give you some praise," he said with a smile.

"Oh, really?"

"Yeah, the wife of the patient in room 240—the one who just had open heart surgery—she said you were taking excellent care of her husband. She couldn't remember your name at first, just said, 'The tall blonde!' I told her, 'That's Chrissy,' and she lit up. 'Oh yes, Chrissy! How could I forget her name?'"

I couldn't help but smile. Moments like that reminded me why I did this work—it wasn't just about meds and monitors. It was about being seen, being felt, and making someone's worst day a little less heavy.

I called Frank on my way home. He said, "I have a surprise for you."

When I got home, Frank took my hand and led me down to the garden. He said, "Chrissy, what do you think?"

Frank had given Bill the task of building me a greenhouse. Bill used some old wood lying around the house and my antique windows, built two long boxes about two feet wide by five feet long, and attached the windows as a roof to protect the young seedlings from the late spring frost.

Bill also put a post in the ground in the corner of the garden and attached my blue birdhouse.

I hugged Frank and said, "You guys are amazing. I love them!"

The next day, we took some of our plants to my grandmother's and my mom's. My grandmother said, "You have my green thumb for growing plants."

I smiled, knowing I was continuing a tradition of growing plants.

Frank and I returned home and placed a layer of straw on the bottom of each box, then began to bring out the vegetable seedlings we had been growing in the attic.

I was reading *Beyond Fear: A Toltec Guide to Freedom and Joy* by Don Miguel Ruiz. Frank knew I was interested in the ancient Toltec ways. He told me about his Lakota Indian friend and said, "You want me to teach you about sweat lodges and the Lakota way?"

I said, "Heck yeah!"

After we finished with the seedlings we crossed the street to the creek and gathered young tree branches that we would bend to form the Inipi–sweat lodge.

We worked all day constructing the inipi. First, we had to find the perfect site to start. We chose the backyard, next to the pavilion, and between the house and the woods.

We dug a hole in the center where the hot stones would be placed, and then carefully bent each branch to form a lodge. The inipi would be large enough to hold six people.

As we bent the branches, each end was hammered deep into the ground, and the next branch was woven between the others. The lodge is formed from 16 young trees or branches to form a circle—a dome. Once the dome was built, we had to cover it with blankets to keep the heat from the rocks inside. One blanket was used to cover the door, which had to face east, and the earth was mounted outside the door. Frank had a massive stack of blankets up in the rafters of the pavilion he used for his ceremonies.

After the inipi was built, we gathered dried grass for the fire and needed to find stones, so Frank took me to the Delaware River the next day.

We woke up and prepared for our adventure. We stopped along the river and walked along the forest's edge, looking for river rocks. Frank asked me if I wanted to see Alice in Wonderland.

I laughed and said, "What is Alice in Wonderland?"

He said, "Old cement train trestles, the locals call Alice in Wonderland. Trust me, I think you will like it."

We arrived at an old train track and parked along the side of the road. Then, we had to climb a small embankment to reach the old train tracks. As we walked across the top of the trestles, graffiti blanketed the cement walls. There were tag signs and random quotes written on the walls.

We approached a manhole carelessly circled in bright red paint and an arrow on the wall across from the hole that pointed down with the words "this way."

I looked down the narrow hole. It was dark, but there was a small light, and you could see the bottom covered in plastic water bottles. I looked at Frank uneasily. He took my hand and said, "You're fine. Go ahead."

I climbed down the manhole into the trestle, which was dark but filled with bright paint. Each side had a U-shaped opening that went up into the cement curvatures that formed the bridge across the river. We entered the opening to the right, which featured the Cheshire cat from Alice in Wonderland painted on it.

"Oh, is this why they call it Alice in Wonderland?" I asked.

He laughed and said, "I guess."

As we climbed the trestles, each room had a U-shaped opening into the next chamber. Each opening revealed different wonders with bright graffiti art. The colors and shapes were mesmerizing. The openings became smaller and smaller, and each chamber shrank until you had to crawl into the very top room.

We dangled our legs over the middle opening of the trestle, looking down at the river, and Frank opened his leather pouch that hung around his neck, pulling out a joint.

It wasn't the first time he smoked pot in front of me. He knew I couldn't smoke pot because I was a nurse. But it didn't stop him.

We sat there as the cool breeze whistled through the tunnels, talking about the preparations for the sweat lodge.

Frank said, "We have built the inipi. Now we will gather our supplies today, fast all day tomorrow, and prepare for the celebration tomorrow night on the full moon."

Frank told me how the Lakota young men were sent into the forest to face their future as warriors. Frank said, "The word Inipi means to live again. The ceremony is a purification rite to help vision quest seekers go on their spiritual rebirth."

A huge smile overtook my entire body, and I thought, *I'm where I belong; I'm ready for a spiritual rebirth.*

It was everything I ever wanted—except I didn't remember wanting it this fast.

Later that day, Tom stopped by for a visit. When he saw me, he looked surprised and said, "Oh, you're still here."

Frank was with one of his school buddies, and they were talking about his music. When I asked what Tom meant by "you're still here," Frank's buddy and Tom both laughed.

Frank tried to change the subject and get them to focus on his music, but Tom said, "You mean, Frank, you didn't tell her about your friend who sold her house and moved in with you and had nowhere to go when you kicked her out?"

Frank hushed Tom up and walked them out to his studio.

Later, I asked him what Tom was talking about.

Frank told me that he used to date this girl he met online. She sold her house and moved in with him, but it just didn't work out. She was crazy, and he had to kick her out.

Frank said, "I never told her to sell her house. She did that on her own. I told her to just rent it out."

I wondered why things didn't work out.

I called Beth later that day to tell her about Tom's comment. Beth said, "Chrissy, you know not everyone is compatible. And people can be crazy. I mean, look, you had to end your two marriages to keep yourself safe. Your first marriage to Joseph was toxic. You had to have him removed with a PFA. And then, Austin, your second marriage, didn't he try to destroy you financially?"

"You're right. I know I'm just worrying too much."

The next day, we prepared for the feast that would follow

Early in the morning, we started the fire.

Frank explained, "The fire represents the sun, and the rocks encircling the fire pit represent the moon, the outer world or cosmos. The lodge represents the inner world, the womb of the mother universe. This is where all souls are created."

Frank continued, "We offer prayers and gifts to our ancestors, the people of the earth." Frank sprinkled tobacco on the rocks and logs.

Frank said, "We offer a prayer of thanks to the universe— Earth, Water, Fire, and Air."

Frank had me pray out loud for my wishes of spiritual awakening as I began my warrior journey.

I prayed to be a gentler, wiser woman. I asked Mother Earth to teach me the warrior's ways, give me the strength to be a better person and mother, and show me how to live my life to benefit others.

I said, "Do you think it would be a good idea for me to pray for my dad's blessings and ask for forgiveness?"

"Yes, Chrissy, that would be an excellent idea. Do you have anything of his?"

"I do." I reached for my necklace. It was a long chain with an arrowhead, my dad had hand-carved out of feldspar, a light orange, hard mineral, and a heart locket with his ashes that my stepmother had gifted me.

"Great."

We spent the day praying and feeding the fire to heat the rocks. We gathered the rest of the supplies. Frank took the buffalo skull from the living room wall and placed it on the mound to the lodge's doorway. We laid my necklace on the skull. Next, he brought out his wooden smoking pipe. The pipe was not like the one my dad used to use. This pipe was long, maybe eighteen inches or more, wrapped in animal hide.

Frank grabbed a metal bucket, which held about two gallons of water. We walked across the street and filled the bucket with cold creek water. When we returned, Frank sat the bucket inside the lodge with a metal ladle hanging from the side.

Frank said, "The ceremony consists of four doors. Each time I open the flap, I will add more rocks, and the heat within the lodge will increase. If at any time you need to leave, just open the door and quietly go."

He continued, "But only a great warrior will complete the four doors and have a full spiritual awakening."

I thought I was being initiated into something ancient.

When the evening approached, Frank said, "The time has come to enter the lodge."

Frank folded the door flap, and we took towels and placed them around the hole in the center of the lodge.

Frank instructed me to sit on the left side of the door. He stated, "Wait here for me and be silent, the only one who speaks is the leader of the ceremony. You can speak when asked a question."

I nodded in agreement.

From inside the lodge, I watched Frank use a pitchfork to gather a few stones and place them inside. Frank then entered the lodge and closed the door flap.

As we sat in a circle, Frank sprinkled dried sage and Frankincense on the rocks. Then he poured a ladle full of water over the stones, filling the lodge with steam. The sweet aroma of the sage and Frankincense filled my lungs.

Frank lit the pipe and prayed to the spirits in his native language.

Frank spoke Lakota words with reverence, but something about it felt rehearsed—like he was wearing a mask carved from someone else's beliefs.

He then passed the pipe to me.

I asked him, "Is there any pot in this pipe?"

He assured me there was none. So, I took a drag.

Frank threw open the flap to the door at the end of each session and returned with more stones each time. He repeated the ritual four more times, and the heat within the lodge became intense with each session, and I thought I would pass out. I knew I had to be strong and endure the heat to become a warrior.

At the end of the fourth session, Frank threw open the door and pronounced, "You may leave, emerge from the dark to the light. All that is impure stays within the lodge."

Although the intensity of the heat and darkness of the lodge were scary, they were truly a spiritual awakening for my entire soul.

The next morning, I woke up feeling fresh—alive in a way I hadn't felt in a while. I headed to work and found myself caring for a man barely in his thirties. He had diabetes, and now, three of his major coronary arteries were nearly 90% blocked. Open-heart surgery wasn't just on the table—it was urgent. Still, he shrugged off a blood sugar of 400 like it was no big deal.

As the cardiologist stood at his bedside, explaining how diabetes silently wrecks the body's major vessels, the Code Blue alarm pierced the air.

Without hesitation, I was at the head of the bed, hands locked, pushing into his chest—counting beats, staying calm. Seconds later, Shawn walked in.

"Need a hand?" he asked.

"We're good, boss. Got it under control," I said without looking up.

I lived for these moments—the chaos, the adrenaline, the split-second clarity. It made me feel powerful, present, and strangely at peace.

I finished my three-day stretch at work..

Frank took me out back and said, "We're going on an adventure today." He pointed to the two bikes sitting by the back porch steps.

I hadn't ridden a bike since I was a kid, and it was exciting. He took me to a big hill; I could only ride halfway up the hill before my legs gave out.

Frank told me, "We can ride a couple of times a week until you master this hill, babe!"

Later that day, Frank said, "I think we need to get bees to pollinate the orchard across the street."

He spoke with a few local beekeepers and ordered a hundred bees and a queen.

Frank purchased all the necessary bee supplies from a farmer friend who had given up on raising bees.

Frank and I placed the beehive stand to the left of the orchard, nestled under the great white pine trees that lined the creek. The next day, we got up early and drove out of town to get our bees.

When we got home, Frank drove his car right up to the hive and put on his beekeeper's suit in preparation for placing the bees in the hive. Frank first took the queen out of her box and placed her into the hive. Then, as if in slow motion, Frank poured the hundreds of bees into the hive. We watched as they swarmed around the queen, protecting her.

The hum of life surrounded us, all seeming to find their place under Frank's careful control.

I told myself this was the beginning of something beautiful. But I couldn't hear the warning signs somewhere in the buzz of it all.

A few days later, Frank brought out his tree-climbing gear, and we spent the day scaling the tree in the backyard. It was playful, almost like a rebirth—just the two of us, high above the ground, free from everything below. I clung to that sense of freedom, but I should have known the shift was coming.

Later that day, we were drinking wine and watching TV. The soft glow of the screen flickered between us, and for a moment, everything felt comfortable, easy—like it was supposed to be.

"You're going to have to start paying rent," he said, his eyes never leaving the screen. "I'm sick of you sponging off me. I've got a bill that's hanging over my head."

I froze, my hand still holding the wine glass. This wasn't the deal. This wasn't what I signed up for. I thought we were building something together. Wasn't I contributing enough? Wasn't my presence enough?

But I didn't say anything. Instead, I nodded, unsure of where the words went, unsure if I was even allowed to ask for more.

My dad was the breadwinner in our family, and my mom didn't work until my sister and I were teenagers. My mom was very submissive to my dad and had to ask for permission to buy things. We grew up poor, but we didn't know the difference as kids. I never went to bed hungry, and we took vacations every summer, camping at the beach.

My sister followed the rules my parents set in our house, while I received a lot of spankings. I challenged the adults, and it usually turned out worse for me. As an adult, I felt ashamed when I was spoken to like a child, and I became angry. I learned to do whatever the other person wanted so that I could avoid feeling like a bad little girl.

I understood Frank had to *dish out* a lot of money in the next few months, but he owned all his apartment buildings and received nearly $15,000 monthly in rental income from his 11 different apartment units. He also owned the house he lived in and did not have a car payment or credit card debt, so *What does he do with all his income*?

I told myself, if he needed help that was the least I could do for him, considering all that he had done for me.

Frank went out the backdoor to the studio and I sat quietly on the edge of the front porch, watching the clouds break apart to reveal a sky that seemed too bright, too hopeful, for the turmoil stirring inside me. The air smelled fresh, almost cleansing, but my chest felt heavy, burdened with thoughts I couldn't yet untangle. Was I still the person I thought I was? Or had I already become something else?

I had once believed that healing came with soft whispers and gentle hands, like the wings of a butterfly emerging from a cocoon. But now, it felt more like I was fighting with monsters—monsters that lurked in the spaces between us, in the things left unsaid, in the chaos disguised as love. The harder I tried to hold on, the more it slipped through my fingers.

The door to the house creaked behind me, and I turned to see Frank standing in the frame, his eyes soft but unreadable.

"I think we need to talk," he said.

He said, "You're saving all this money living with me and not helping me. I think it's about time Frank benefited from a woman moving in with him."

And just like that, I knew the real storm was coming and I'd be up all night.

# Chapter 6

## Monsters And Butterflies

Spring flew by.

We woke up after a terrible thunderstorm passed through overnight. We inspected the garden, and Frank had forgotten to close the greenhouse windows. The windows were lying half on the wooden frame and half on the ground, and a few of the glass panes were shattered. Frank grabbed the window and started tearing and ripping at the frame with the force of a grizzly bear. The window popped off, and he threw it with all his might to the ground and glass shattered on the lawn.

The glass shattered like my illusion of control that everything was fine.

Frank's fury seemed almost too big for the world, like it could swallow me whole, yet I stood frozen, unable to piece it together. *Why don't I say anything?*

We wandered across the street to check on the bees. A bear had gotten into the hive and torn it apart. Frank started screaming, "I can't have anything nice without someone or something destroying it!"

I finally found my voice. "Baby, we can fence around the hive. Remember the old man we got the hive from who told us to put a fence up because of the bears."

Frank stood there staring at the hive sprawled across the grass and than turned around and said, "Chrissy, you are so smart; this is why I love you so much. You are right. We will do that tomorrow."

Tomorrow came and went, and the bear returned two more times and destroyed the hive. The last time the bear returned, the hive was ripped into pieces. Frank never put up the fence.

I told myself it was just a window. Just a bear. Not the end of the world.

But deep down, a knot tightened in my chest every time I let it slide—every time I ignored the signs.

Was I overreacting? Being paranoid? Or was something truly off?

I didn't tell any of my friends what happened. I had learned, as a child to stay quiet about horrible things. When you speak up, people look at you differently. Like you're broken. Like you're tainted.

So I buried it—just like I always had.

When I moved in back in March, I had shown Frank some of my drawings from college and told him that I loved to paint and dabbled in watercolor painting with a few friends at our local art center. I told Frank that my dad used to paint. He drew murals for our local middle school that were in the cafeteria, and he painted oil pictures for my mom and a few friends. I laughed and said, "My grandmother said I'm like my dad and am overflowing with talent."

Frank found out that the church down the street was offering watercolor classes and offered to pay for it for me.

Frank said, "You pay for the class. I'll pay you back.

I signed up, paid for the class, and bought the needed supplies.

My first session went well. I came home, and Frank raved about how amazing my painting was and looked forward to more progress.

The following week, I went to my class and struggled a bit with blending colors, but the instructor encouraged me to practice more at home. I spent that week following the instructor's suggestions, and when it came time to go to my next session, Frank said, "Baby, maybe painting isn't for you. I don't want you to keep embarrassing yourself, so I'll tell you the truth. Your paintings are terrible."

I looked down at my drawings and said, "Really, my instructor told me they were excellent. I just needed to practice blending my colors."

Frank said, "He gets paid by the people who attend his class. I'm sorry, but these drawings are just awful. You lack artistic talent."

Without thinking, I tore the paper in half, leaped up, and, with a heavy heart, stomped into the kitchen and out the back door to the dumpster.

With the force of a gorilla I heaved everything over the top–including my college drawings and supplies.

Frank said, "Don't be so hard on yourself. Not everyone can be a Picasso."

Frank tearing apart my paintings felt like a direct attack on everything I thought I loved about myself. My hands shook as I wondered if maybe he was right. But my instructor had seen promise. Why did I choose his words over my own? And why did I throw everything away, as if it was all just a lie?

I never went back to my painting classes, and Frank never reimbursed me for the class.

Frank spent a lot of time in his studio trying to form a new band, while I spent my days off in the garden or having tea with my grandmother.

One morning, Frank was sitting on the back porch and said, "Chrissy, I know you used to have chickens, and I was thinking we should get a few for the backyard."

I ran over to him and said, "Yes, Chickens will be great at eating the bugs in the yard, and we can use the chicken manure in the garden–besides, fresh eggs are the best!"

When I lived next to my grandmother, I had chickens. I had a beautiful Plymouth Rock rooster, as well as Americana, Red Sex Link, Brahma, and Rhode Island Red Hens. I bought an egg incubator and hatched my Americana babies myself. Americana chicks are also known as the Easter egg chicken; they lay eggs in shades of pink, green, and blue.

Frank and I hastily cleaned up the back shed and put up a fence in preparation for new little friends.

The chickens felt like a fresh start, a little joy in the midst of everything. But, as always, the excitement faded once I realized that Frank had planted the idea, and now it was another way of pulling me into his world of chaos. Maybe that's what he was really offering— more of my life that I would sacrifice for a dream that wasn't real— more empty promises.

Like the headboard on our bed and my photography classes—tomorrow. But, for some promises Frank made, tomorrow never came.

Frank had finished rehabbing the apartment next door, and a couple had moved in. It was good to have someone to talk to during the day when Frank was not around.

It was also nice to have someone else see what was happening between Frank and me.

I distinctly remember the first time he scolded me in a voice that felt almost paternally supportive yet charged with condescension. He looked at me with an intensity that made my heart race and declared,

"I'm not speaking to you for the rest of the day. I do not like the way you treat me."

Initially, I thought he was joking; its ridiculousness made me laugh nervously. But his expression indicated he was deadly serious. It became painfully clear to me that this was not just a threat but a form of punishment that would go on to shape my understanding of love and control in ways I could never have anticipated. The reality of that moment was more terrifying than I had ever imagined, and it marked the beginning of a journey that would leave me questioning my own worth and losing my voice and my entire self as I fell deeper and deeper into despair.

Even though I sensed, deep down, that something was off, I couldn't help but feel an initial pull towards him. How could this man, standing before me now, unleash such cruel words with such ease? I reflected on the man I had met just a few months ago; he had seemed so kind and gentle.

One minute, Frank could be sweet, loving, and charming, but the next, he would lash out in ways that left me reeling. I started questioning myself more—was I imagining it? Had I done something wrong? I couldn't remember who he had been when I first met him, or if he'd ever been that person at all.

Frank would lash out, saying, "You make me sick just being near me," and repeatedly scream, "Get the fuck out of my house!"

With every cruel word, I felt myself shrinking. The woman I thought I was—strong, independent, creative—seemed to vanish a little more each day. Who was I now? What had I become in his eyes? Was I just the woman who would take his abuse and still come back for more?

As if in a trance, I walked towards the door, and he would say, "I knew it. You're just like all the others; you don't care about me."

The silence between us grew thick, heavy. I could hear my heart pounding in my chest, feel my breath quicken. I was seeing the cracks in the foundation of everything I had built around us. But I was too afraid to acknowledge it, too afraid to lose him. So, I stayed. But the cost was becoming too high. Somewhere deep inside, I knew I couldn't keep pretending anymore. This was no longer love—it was control, it was manipulation, it was suffocation.

# Chapter 7

## The Mirror Room

The mirror doesn't lie. It reflects what you've tried to hide—the bruises no one sees, the truth you keep swallowing, the woman you no longer recognize.

We were still riding bikes every week. I had mastered the hill, but as we rode home one day, Frank said, "Chrissy, I think you need to cut back on the sweets. You're getting a fat roll on your back."

I immediately stopped my bike and grabbed my back fat. I was 5'7" tall and weighed maybe 132 pounds, and I said, "You think so, baby?"

Frank laughed and said, "Well, I'm just being honest. I think maybe you should watch what you're eating. It's probably my fault—all those late-night snacks while we watch movies."

In middle school, I barely ate anything and weighed 118 pounds. I had told Frank how I suffered from anorexia growing up and how I weighed myself weekly and worked out every day.

I told myself he was being honest. He said this because he knew how important I took my weight. It was because he loved me.

One day, Frank's friend came to the house and asked where Frank was.

"Frank just ran out to run a few errands."

His friend said, "Oh, I'll wait here. He told me to stop by."

We sat at the kitchen table talking when Frank came back. He slammed the back door and came into the kitchen. He asked what was going on.

His friend said, "Hey, you asked me to stop by today."

"Oh, yeah, I did. Let's head out to the studio."

When his friend left, Frank came back into the house and said, "I can't even trust you. Were you flirting with my friend? I heard you two laughing when I came into the house."

Frank said, "You better not be trying to hook up with my friends. I'll throw you the fuck out of my house."

*Maybe I did laugh too loud. Maybe I should've gone upstairs. Was I too friendly?*

I looked at Frank and said, "What? Oh, my God, no. He said you told him to stop by and that he would wait for you to come back. I was just talking to him."

I was starting to question how I got to this point. Why did I move out of my house and move in with him?

One day I was Frank's everything; the next day, he was screaming, "Get the fuck out!"

The neighbor next door started asking me if everything was okay between Frank and me because she could hear him yelling at me through the walls.

I felt like I was losing my mind and that I was utterly powerless and trapped. Every single day was like walking on eggshells, never knowing what might trigger him.

I pretended to my friends that Frank and I were amazing together.

I stopped inviting my friends and family over because Frank hated every one of them.

He said, "You deserve better friends."

Frank didn't like my family either. "I don't think your kids respect you, and your mom doesn't like me."

My support system was shriveling, and I was too ashamed to tell my grandmother what was happening at home.

I used to talk to the neighbor, Lynne, but Frank told me, "Keep your mouth shut to the neighbors because they tell me everything you say about me."

Frank opened a bottle of wine that night, and we sat and drank. Every time my glass was empty, he filled it. I told him, "I work tomorrow."

He said, "Relax a bit, baby."

After he opened the second bottle of wine, we started to fight. "You know what, Chrissy? You're a feral woman, and I need to know I can trust you with my friends."

"Baby, I wasn't flirting with your friend. Please, I have to work tomorrow."

"I don't care if you have to work. You cannot treat me this way. I demand respect. You live in my house, and I will not have a fucking whore living with me."

I spent most of the night crying and begging Frank to let me sleep. Trying to block his voice out. By the time morning came around, I was emotionally drained.

Frank said, "I'm done. I'm going to sleep in the other room. You disgust me."

I had missed too many days already with Frank and me fighting. Calling out was not an option.

I got up and got ready for work.

Driving to work, I thought, *What am I doing?*

I finally broke down. I walked into work, and one of my friends grabbed my arm and asked me if I was okay.

Her voice sounded far away. My body felt like it wasn't mine anymore. When I came to, I was in my manager's office and Shawn was there too.

I opened up about everything. Shawn talked me down. I was not thinking straight.

My manager called security, and we set up an appointment that day with the Women's Crisis Center for battered women.

Everything happened so fast. There was little time to think. Next thing I knew I was sitting in an office telling a stranger about my nightmare of a life. It felt like I was talking about another person's life.

I was not that woman; I was strong and independent. I had a career; I didn't need a man in my life.

The woman sitting across from me leaned in towards me and said, "Do you think you're weak?"

I said, "I don't know what I am anymore."

She said, "I sat right where you are two years ago. I met a man who loved me like a queen, and without warning, I found myself sneaking out with nothing but a duffel bag filled with my things."

She continued, "You see, abuse doesn't care if you are strong or weak....It can affect anyone. At any time."

"Now let's find you someplace safe to live."

The woman helped me find an apartment that was available immediately.

Luck was on my side!

That afternoon, I went home and told Frank, "Things just aren't working out. I need to move out."

He just looked at me and asked, "Do you need help packing your things?"

He even offered to give me the red dresser I loved. He wanted to keep the rug I bought for his living room and my antique dressers.

He said, "I know you will be back, babe. But you do what you need to for now."

It was June, six months since I met Frank, two months since I moved in with him, and the first time I packed my things and left.

The woman I was, was gone. The one walking out—she had a long way to go, but at least she was walking away.

> The worst loneliness is to not be
> comfortable with yourself. — Mark Twain

# Chapter 8

## Broken Wings

I didn't cry while packing, but the silence screamed louder than any fight we ever had.

My friends Beth, Kelly, and Dave agreed to help move me out. Eric, who was dating Kelly, came along to help them.

Frank was quiet and didn't fight with me, but he did take Eric aside to talk to him. I heard their muffled yelling, but I couldn't make out what they were saying.

Eric came back, and we finished loading up my things.

The apartment I found was an old Victorian house that had been divided into two units, one at the bottom and one at the top. I rented the two-bedroom unit upstairs. It was perfect and within walking distance of my job. The apartment had off-street parking in the back. I had never lived in an apartment building before, but it was very convenient and affordable.

Every room had huge windows to let in the sunlight. I spent days decorating and arranging my furniture to make the place feel like home.

Dave, my neighbor from the community where I owned my house, was such an amazing friend of mine, and what luck—he worked right down the street from my new apartment. This worked out because I needed someone to walk my doggie in the afternoon on the days I worked. Leaving little Daizy alone in the house for thirteen hours felt unthinkable—she'd been my shadow through everything.

I kept crying in the shower, at work, in the car. Therapy felt like the only lifeline.

The counselor at the Women's Crisis Center listened quietly. I didn't even have to say much before the shame spilled out.

A few weeks later, my friends nudged me toward dating—maybe to distract me, maybe to remind me I still existed beyond Frank.

I went on a date with this guy, he was nice. He liked to ride bikes. He took me to pick out a bike and went riding on the trails a few times.

But I wasn't ready to move on.

Frank's ex-girlfriend Stacy messaged me to say she heard I had moved out. Of course, she did; they talked the whole time Frank and I were together.

I don't know why, but Stacy and I exchanged phone numbers and chatted about how Frank treated her. She said she was glad I had left.

Stacy told me about Frank's girlfriend before her. She lived in another state, and Frank and she were talking, and he asked her to move in with him. She had sold all her things for the move, and after just three months, he kicked her out, and she was homeless. I asked what happened to her, and Stacy said, "She ended up moving to California to live with her parents the last I had heard."

Stacy told me Frank begged her to move in with him, but she refused.

I told Stacy about the clothes and stuff I found in the closet. She said, "Yeah, Frank has a habit of getting women to move in with him and then kicking them out when they go crazy. I know I left a few things there, but I wouldn't step foot in that house if you paid me to."

I wish I hadn't moved in with Frank. I had a cute house, and my life had been going pretty well.

I felt I was getting stronger.

Going to therapy, learning about toxic relationships. Maybe I could stand on my own two feet. But then I met this guy from down the road from me, and we started meeting on my front porch and drinking wine.

Alcohol is a bad decision when you have a broken heart.

That night, I poured my story into a stranger's glass—the hurt, the confusion, the leftover pieces of me I hadn't figured out how to carry alone.

I drank too much. Said too much. Felt too much.

Then I ran inside and called Frank.

I may have physically left Frank's house, but Frank's poison was coursing through my veins—I failed. I invited him over to visit.

The next day, Frank came to my apartment, and we went out to eat lunch. We agreed to take it slow. Frank said, "I'll need you to treat me better if you move in. I have to know I can trust you and not hurt me." He continued, "I'm so embarrassed that you packed up and left. I'm not sure how I feel about you moving back in with me. What will the neighbors say? What will my friends think about me?"

I said, "I'm not moving back in. We can date for a while and see how things go."

I started seeing a new therapist. We began to unpack pieces of my past—fractured relationships, childhood trauma, the stories I had told myself just to survive. After three weeks, we had barely scratched the surface. But one conversation stuck with me: we were discussing the cycle of toxic abuse when she casually mentioned the word narcissism.

That night, I looked it up—and froze. The traits were a near-perfect match for Frank. Each one felt like a puzzle piece snapping into place. I couldn't believe Frank was this evil. *How could this be?*

I knew I still needed therapy and finding the right therapist is one of the hardest parts of healing. The woman I'd been seeing was kind, even insightful, but I needed more. I needed someone who could peel back the layers, who wouldn't let me hide behind my lies or let me get away with denying the truth. I didn't just want to be heard—I needed to be seen, to be challenged.

But starting over felt like hell. I hated having to go back to the beginning—recounting the mundane, messy details of my messed-up life. Still, I showed up to my first appointment with a new counselor, nerves tangled in my gut. I began to explain my situation with Frank, the confusion, the fear.

She looked at me and said, "Are you fucking stupid? You left and then you told him where you lived?"

Her words landed harder than anything Frank had ever said. I wasn't just embarrassed—I was shattered. My stomach twisted. I couldn't breathe. I nodded silently, stood up, and walked out.

In the car, I didn't even cry. I just sat there, frozen. My whole body swallowed up in shame.

I called my friend Beth and told her what happened. Her voice, calm and fierce, was a lifeline.

"Oh, honey," she said. "We all do what we think is right in the moment. You'll see he's not right for you in time—

but that woman had no business speaking to you that way. You need to report her. You walked into her office afraid, vulnerable, trying to open up, and she attacked you. That's not just unprofessional—it's cruel."

She paused, then added, "Find a new therapist. One that's right for you."

She was right—I wasn't ready to walk away from Frank yet, but that didn't make me stupid. It just made me human. I took a breath, found a new therapist, and made another appointment for the following week.

This time, I prayed it would be different.

A few days later, Frank came over. I showed him my new bike and told him I was starting my nurse practitioner program in August.

He smiled and said, "I like your bike, and good for you—reaching your goals."

I didn't go back that night.

I didn't go back the next week.

My wings were still broken—I knew I had to mend them myself.

It was now the beginning of August and he stopped by.

"I have a surprise for you today." He took me out of town to show me a bookstore filled with used books. He knew I loved books, and his kindness so touched me. Afterward, we went out to eat at a fancy restaurant. He told me he used to take Stacy there; she lived nearby but never liked the food.

Frank looked at me, grabbed my hand, and said, "Baby, come home, where you belong with me. The chickens miss you, the garden is a mess without you, and it's time to make a new batch of Kombucha."

He wasn't talking about chickens. Or gardens. He was talking about control. And for a moment, I forgot the cost of going back.

*Just when I thought I was airborne, I crashed into the old lie: that he'd changed, that we were different now.*

> The people you meet are either reflections of a
> repeated cycle or guides towards a new start.
> Notice the difference. — Chantel Jones

# Chapter 9

## Eating Leftovers, Again

August. Another box. Another promise. The third time I'd packed my things since meeting Frank, and just like the times before, I told myself this time would be different. But you can't rewrite history—you can only dress it in new clothes. And no matter how you style it, it's still the same old shit.

When Kelly found out I was moving back in with Frank, she didn't hold back.

"You're a fucking idiot," she said—and then she cut me out of her life completely.

My mom just shook her head. "He's going to kill you. What are you doing?"

I withdrew from college. I told myself Frank loved me. That if I could just be better—more patient, more understanding, less emotional—everything would work. The fight had been my fault. Hadn't it?

I started seeing a new therapist named Judy. We didn't talk about Frank, not at first. She didn't pry. Instead, she asked me about me—my goals, my passions, the things that made me feel alive. I liked that. I felt comfortable around her.

I told her how I loved to draw and paint. How journaling had been my lifeline for as long as I could remember—my safe space when everything else was chaos.

"That's good," she said. "We can incorporate journaling into your sessions."

Then she asked about my childhood.

I offered bits and pieces. Fractured memories. Edges of truth dulled by time and survival. But then one memory burst through—sharp and suffocating. That night in the bathroom. My father's fingers around my neck.

I couldn't breathe.

I was fifteen again. Screaming. Flying. Then slamming into the wall.

I had been getting ready to go out with friends—makeup half done, music playing. My mom said I wasn't allowed to go, and I snapped back, "I'm going."

Then I heard it—heavy footsteps coming down the hall.

My father's voice, low and dangerous: "You're not going anywhere."

I walked out of the bathroom, looked at him, and screamed, "I'm fucking going out!"

Without even a moment of hesitation, my dad grabbed me around my neck, slammed my head through the sheetrock, and held me with my feet dangling above the floor.

In another session, I recalled my first abusive romantic relationship.

My first boyfriend almost put me in the hospital on my fourteenth birthday.

I was at his house, and he started yelling at me, and I yelled back. He punched me in the face right in front of his mom. She tried to stop him, but he punched her too. I ran out of the house with him chasing me.

He grabbed me and started punching me. I spit in his face as he kicked me over and over again. His dad came out of the house and stopped him. I jumped up and started running. I just kept running. I finally stopped in the middle of the woods and cried.

Judy asked me, "Why did you run? What did you want to happen in that moment?"

I told her, "I wanted someone to save me, someone to find me...tell me I was safe."

But I didn't even know where I had run off to. I started walking until I found a road. I followed the road back home. When I opened the door, my mom asked me what had happened.

I sat down and told her everything. She looked at my dad and said, "We have to call the police."

*Yes! Stick up for me. Show me I'm worth something, that you care about me.*

My dad said, "No. We will call his mom and dad and keep them away from each other."

I thought, *Chrissy, you're not worth their time or the police's time. You're no one and nothing.*

One of the most eye-opening sessions we had was when I told Judy that, when I was a teenager, my mom had a friend who was a psychologist, and I started seeing her. I didn't understand why my mom sent me; I thought it was to make her look like a good mom.

Judy encouraged me to write about my therapy sessions with my mom's friend. When I went back to Judy the next week and read my journal entry, it was more about what I didn't talk about with my old therapist.

> Journal Entry: I never told the therapist that my uncle used to come to the house when no one was home and touch my breasts. He said, "It's okay. Don't tell your mom or dad. Your mom lets me touch her too."
>
> I never told my therapist that when I was scared, I would hide in the attic, in the kitchen cabinets, or in my closet with a pile of clothes on top of me. I never told her that I smoked pot in the girls' bathroom every day and that I threatened to kill Mindy, the girl who stole my boyfriend from the roller rink.
>
> I didn't even tell her that when I was thirteen, I took a handful of aspirin and prayed I would die.

I didn't tell her my sister and aunt used to make fun of me because I couldn't spell and would tell me I was a mistake—a backseat special. My aunt said, "Ya' know your mom and dad only got married because your mom got pregnant with you." She said, "Ya' know you ruined a lot of people's lives, and you are nothing but a disappointment. No one cares about you, and I wish you were never born."

Instead, of writing down these things or telling about them to that therapist, I was a good little girl. I did my journaling exercises. I would tell her, "I want to be a lawyer or a psychologist like you when I grow up."

Judy asked, "How did this make you feel writing it out?"

I said, "Inside, the anger was growing. I couldn't tell her my darkest fears—she was my mom's best friend."

Back then, my parents didn't know what to do with me. I was smoking cigarettes in the house, sneaking out at night, smoking pot, and coming home drunk. I came home one day, and they sat me down and told me they were sending me to an all-girls school in New York. I figured they were tired of dealing with me, so I decided I'd make it easier and more cost-effective for them.

After everyone went to bed that night, I packed a bag and ran away.

I ran away to my ex-boyfriend's house, but his mom called my parents. When I got home, my dad sat in his den chair. I looked at him, and his eyes were all bloodshot. He didn't say a word to me. I thought he looked like he was crying back then, but I think he was more worried about his reputation than my well-being.

Mom thanked my ex-boyfriend's parents for bringing me home, and she told me I was grounded and didn't know what she was going to do with me.

She didn't say anything else. She just walked away. She didn't have to. Her silence and dismissal of the events screamed enough.

In my head I heard—*You are embarrassing this family with your behavior.*

I'm sure my mom did her best to keep my boyfriend and me apart, but it didn't work. I stayed away from him for most of high school, but he called the summer after eleventh grade and asked if I wanted to see him. I knew that I shouldn't, but I said yes. Within a few months, I was pregnant.

In my family it seemed like everyone turned a blind eye to the abusive husbands and who was sleeping with whom.

After my boyfriend and I got married, my aunt, who lived near my grandmother, offered to sell us her house. She no longer lived there and had rented it out. I was thrilled that we would be so close to my grandmother.

However, my paternal grandfather suddenly passed away, and the world I knew began to change dramatically.

I was 19 when my parents divorced. I didn't think I would take it as hard as I did. But I was hurt. Even though, as a teenager, I had wished for their divorce, it was still my family and the chaos I had grown accustomed to.

My dad, my uncle (yeah, the creepy one), and my husband spent the summer and fall of 1987 rehabbing the house, adding a new addition to the back, installing new flooring, updating the wiring, fixing the plumbing, and installing a new roof. It was a lot of work, but it would become our home.

My mom discovered that my dad was moving his new girlfriend into our family home. She told me, "I always knew your dad was cheating, and I would have stayed and let him keep his girlfriend just to keep our family together."

The first time I tried to leave my first husband, my dad said, "Wait until the kids are grown; things all change then."

My grandmother told me, "Be a better wife, and he won't hit you."

I continued to see Judy. But I never told her I was going back to Frank. I couldn't say it out loud. Saying it would mean admitting that I was choosing him again— choosing the pain. And even though my mouth stayed shut, my silence was screaming.

It wasn't love I was chasing—it was familiarity. And familiarity, no matter how rotten, always tasted like home. Even if it was just leftovers.

Narcissistic love is riding on the
rollercoaster of disaster filled with a
heart full of tears. — Sheree Griffin

# Chapter 10

## Shattered Dreams

Some dreams die quietly. Others go up in flames, splintered and smoking in the backyard while you stand there pretending it doesn't hurt. This was the second kind.

Frank offered to pay for the U-Haul, and he and Bill helped me pack my things—one more time.

As we unloaded the U-Haul, Frank said he didn't want to store my antique furniture anymore.

The Victorian couch I'd always dreamed of owning. The China hutch passed down from my first mother-in-law. The pieces of a life I had built before him—he wanted them gone.

I had always wanted a Victorian claw-foot couch, and my second husband and I found one that perfectly matched my antique lamps in the living room.

The hutch was a gift from my first mother-in-law; it belonged to her mother.

With all the anger festering in my body, I told Frank, "Fine, let's just burn the shit!"

We built a bonfire in the backyard. Frank took a sledgehammer to the couch and broke it into two pieces. He tossed it into the fire. I watched in horror as the flames engulfed the couch within seconds. Frank grabbed the antique desk chair I had reupholstered and threw it on top of the burning couch. He turned to the other half of the sofa and smashed the bottom frame into slivers with a bone-jarring crash.

The flames rose high, devouring the velvet and wood like it had always been waiting for this moment. I stood frozen as springs flew through the air like shooting stars.

There go my dreams, I thought, falling from the sky— shattering into a million pieces across the lawn.

That couch wasn't just furniture. It was a version of me who once believed in home, comfort, beauty. Watching it burn felt like proof that I didn't deserve those things anymore.

Frank asked me to help him throw the hutch into the fire.

"Can we wait? I'm gonna ask my mom if she can store the hutch for me."

"Sure, just help me get it off the truck."

As we took the hutch off the truck, Frank dropped his end, and one of the glass panes cracked. Frank said, "Oh, Chrissy. I'm sorry. I'll fix it tomorrow, I promise."

The whole episode felt like a nightmare. I spent years studying for my degree. I worked my ass off to buy a house, and here I was, burning the things I held dearest to my heart.

The following day I woke up, I laid in bed staring at the ceiling and thought, *I fucked up.*

I dragged myself out of bed; Frank was still sleeping; I didn't want to wake him. I grabbed Daizy, slowly pulled the bedroom door closed, and snuck down the hallway. I tiptoed down the stairs and into the kitchen. I grabbed a cold cup of coffee that was left in the pot and took Daizy outside. Standing on the back porch, I closed my eyes and took a deep breath. The air was filled with the smell of soot and lingering smoke. *Oh, yeah, I burnt my life last night.* I wandered over to the smoldering ashes, and there, among them lay the remains of my old life. Tears rolled down my face as I stared at the couch springs and screws, and drawer pulls. *Chrissy, breathe, just breathe.*

I heard the coffee grinder in the house—Frank was up.

I didn't want to go back to the house. I wasn't ready to face my mistake.

The back door opened, and Frank yelled, "You want to go for a bike ride down by the river?"

"Heck, ya!"

I mentioned to Frank that my therapist and I agreed I shouldn't drink anymore.

Frank replied, "I think that's a great idea."

Once we got to the park, we unloaded our bikes, checked the tire pressure, and began our ride. A few minutes later, he asked about the guy I dated after moving out. I didn't want to discuss it, but he kept asking questions.

I told Frank that the guy had taken me to pick out this bike. We had ridden a few times.

Frank got mad and started riding faster. He left me behind, and when I tried to catch up, I didn't know which trail he had taken. I turned around and went back to the car. I knew that no matter what I did, I would get in trouble; it wasn't the answer he was looking for.

About an hour later, he returned, yelling at me, "Where did you go? You just left me!"

I tried to explain that I couldn't catch up and lost him.

He replied, "I knew I should have never given you another chance and let you move back in with me."

That night, Frank didn't want to talk. He went out to his studio. I messaged Shawn from work on Facebook, and we chatted about my mom and dad and the people I needed to forgive. He told me about John Grey's "The Feeling Letter"—a process where you write a letter to the person you're upset with, then write a response to yourself as if you were that person. The final step is writing a letter back to them, saying goodbye and forgiving them.

I thought, *Yes, I read about something similar years ago. But there was a fourth step: You would go outside and burn the letters, fully releasing the feelings and letting go.*

I had already burned something sacred and didn't feel lighter. I didn't feel free. I felt hollow.

Maybe I didn't need to forgive. Maybe I needed to finally grieve. For my dreams. For my younger self. For the version of me I set on fire just to feel loved.

Frank promised me change. He promised me love. But promises are debts that always come due. And every promise he made to me, I paid for in pieces of shattered dreams across the lawn.

# Chapter 11

## Dancing With The Devil

I used to think love was loud laughter in the sun, framed photos on the wall, and spontaneous kisses after a night of music. But I was wrong. Love shouldn't come with bruised egos, broken glass, and a heart that flinches when a dish rack hits the ceiling.

Frank knew how to make life feel like a movie—until the credits rolled, and the lights came up. Then all that was left was the mess on the floor, and me, trying to sweep it up with bleeding feet.

Frank could be so helpful and kind at times. He had a bookshelf in the corner of the living room, and I told him I needed to find a good book to read.

He suggested, "Why don't you read *Tracks*?"

"What's it about?"

"It's about a woman who travels across the desert with an Australian tribe."

"Why not?"

Frank bent over, grabbed the book from the shelf, and handed it to me.

We spent hours in our lawn chairs in the backyard, soaking up the sun as I read the book. The book took me across deserts and into dreams—places where women walked away, free and unafraid. I devoured every word, intoxicated by the idea of disappearing into a world where no one could ever hurt me again.

Frank laughed at me when I mentioned exploring the world. "Chrissy, you've never lived anywhere but your little hometown."

*I know, but one day I will get out of this fucking little town.*

Frank started playing at a local bar, so I invited Beth and Dave, who still kept in touch with me, to come along and watch him perform. The bar was small and loud. The three of us wandered through the crowd until we reached a booth right up front by the band. It was such an exhilarating night, filled with live music, friends, and a world I had never experienced before. I was the lead singer's girlfriend!

As the guys were packing up their equipment, a man approached me and asked about the band. I was excited to tell him about the next place Frank was going to play at, and I told the guy about Frank's YouTube channel. Frank came back in and saw me talking to the man, grabbed me by the waist, swept me off my feet, swung me around, and then kissed me.

I thought we had an amazing time until we got in the car, and Frank asked, "Who was that guy you were talking to over by the bar?"

"Oh, he asked me about your band and where all you played."

Tires screeched. My body lurched forward. Dust encased the car as we hit the shoulder of the road.

"You were flirting!" he spat.

I blinked, heart racing. "What? No, I—"

"Don't lie to me." His voice cracked like a whip. "You better not embarrass me and flirt right in front of my friends and me."

My hands trembled. I reached for his, a reflex. Stupid. He yanked it away like I'd burned him.

The air between us turned thick.

And just like that, the night turned into something I'd need to survive.

The summer was a whirlwind of late nights, campfires in the backyard, bike riding, and sweat lodges.

Frank and I returned to Alice in Wonderland with a friend from work. The three of us sat looking out over the river. My friend looked at us and said, "You guys look amazing together."

Frank teased that we should take engagement photos, and in that moment, under graffiti-splashed tunnels glowing with filtered sunlight, I believed him. We posed like lovers in a storybook—smiling, playful, caught in a snapshot of make-believe where nothing was broken and everything still held promise.

A few of the pictures turned out so well that I had them printed, and we framed and hung them in the living room.

After Alice, we all went out for lunch at a bar near the river and spent hours shooting pool before heading home. It was an incredible day.

But the good never lasted more than two or three days.

Frank took me to a local swimming hole known as Red Rock. We parked across the street from a golf course, hiked about a quarter of a mile into the woods, crossed a train track, and descended an embankment to reach the stream. There was a rock ledge with a rope swing and a bridge where a few people stood, and we watched them jump into the water.

I took pictures of the graffiti on the bridge, and on the way back to the train, we could hear one coming in the distance. I grew up visiting my aunt in the city, where she lived across from a train track. I remember how the whole house shook at night when the trains passed. As the train got closer, I lay on the grass about two feet from the track and recorded a video. Frank laughed and said, "Chrissy, you are such a wild woman."

My cell phone was filled with videos and pictures of all our adventures. I uploaded a few of them, but not everything.

Later that afternoon, we stood in the kitchen. I was searching for a dinner recipe. Frank said, "Why are you always on your phone? Why don't you find what you need in a book?"

One second, it was in my hands. The next ...smash.

Glass flew—plastic split.

I backed away, my fists clenched.

"My pictures," I whispered. "The train. The—"

"Memories are in your head," he snapped.

And then he walked out, leaving silence louder than any scream.

I clung to the shattered phone, my knees shaking, head heavy, filled with regret, and flopped into a chair.

Holding onto what was left of my broken life.

When he returned, he said, "Such a long face. I'll take you and buy you a new phone. I also want to put a hitch on your car. This way, our bikes will be secure for our rides."

Frank bought me a new phone and installed the hitch on my car, but it didn't change who he was.

All the memories were gone. The phone was in two pieces. There was no backup—like my life, no backup plan.

Just one moment away from being erased.

A couple of days later, I was in the kitchen and asked if we could go to the county fair the next week.

"The fair is for entertaining the uneducated," Frank said. "I have no desire to lower myself and partake in that circus."

The county fair happened in the last week of August, and I had never missed a year. I begged him, "Oh, baby, please. I love walking around and seeing the animals. And ya' know they have waffles and ice cream."

He picked up the dish drying rack from the sink and threw it straight up in the air. It hit the ceiling, and the dishes fell like gold ball-sized hail. Shattered glass and broken plastic came crashing down all around my bare feet.

Frank screamed, "Get the fuck out of my house."

I picked up my dog and, in a fog, walked towards the back door. As I reached for the doorknob, I heard a woosh as a head of cabbage smashed off the door frame, missing my head by a mere thread.

Frank started to cry and told me I was just like all the other women.

I just sat down on the porch step, clutching my dog like a life raft, surrounded by the debris of my dreams.

I looked up. Chickens were grazing in the grass, picking up bugs between the broken glass of the greenhouse window, and leaning against the garage door. Their little feet were clicking against the faded box from my Christmas tree that never made it into the house.

And there was my antique China cabinet with the veneer peeling off from being in the rain.

The cabbage rolled slowly to a stop in the grass. I stared at it, stunned that something so absurd could nearly take my life.

And just like that, the illusion cracked again.

But my rose-colored glasses were still on.

I needed to be gentler.

*Why did I push him when he said no?*

*Scars are not shameful, not unless you let them be. If you do not wear them, they will wear you. — V. E. Schwab*

# Chapter 12

## Shameful Little Girl

The trees were shedding their leaves—letting go with quiet grace. I envied them. Autumn has always been my favorite season, but this year, it feels more like a silent funeral. One for the parts of myself I had long buried under bruises, silence, and shame.

Somehow, I mustered up the courage to plan a trip to Oregon to visit my youngest daughter, and I was taking my oldest daughter with me. It was another mother-daughter vacation.

Frank didn't say much about my plans. "Chrissy, I think it will be good for you to get away for a bit. You know, see more of the world."

I seldom escaped from the house without Frank asking me, "Where are you going? How long will you be gone? Are you sure you're going there and not just going to hook up with someone?"

I had been going to the same salon for a few years and built a friendship with Liz. Every five to eight weeks, I would go to get my highlights and have my roots touched up.

I told Frank I was leaving for my appointment.

He didn't say a word.

Most of the time, Frank left me alone. It was just down the street, and he knew where it was. But sometimes, I would sit in the chair and hear him say, "Hey, is Chrissy here? Oh, there you are, baby." He'd walk into the salon and kiss me in my chair.

At first, I thought it was cute, but the cuteness wore off, and it started to feel more like stalking.

As I sat in the salon, I barely spoke a word. I was so numb and confused.

My hairdresser, Liz, looked at me and asked, "What's wrong with you?"

I was staring at the floor, and without lifting my head, I replied, "Nothing."

It was a hot day; Indian summer had arrived, and I was wearing a long-sleeved shirt.

She grabbed my arms and pulled the sleeves of my shirt up. I had bruises all up and down my arms from Frank grabbing and shaking me every time he yelled at me.

Liz said, "What are you doing? You have dark circles under your eyes, you're not wearing any makeup, and you look terrible!"

I looked down at the floor and said, "One second, he's amazing, and then, in a split second...he's throwing my things out the door." I looked up at her, and she handed me a box of tissues. I said, "He screams like he wants to rip the walls down. 'Get the fuck out of my house!' And then—just like that—he's on his knees, begging me to stay. Crying. Telling me I'm all he has left.

"What am I supposed to do? ...Should I walk out and leave him? Or should I show him I'm not like everyone else? I'm so fucking lost. I don't even know who I am anymore."

Liz said, "What does your therapist say you should do?"

"I haven't told her I'm back with Frank. She thinks I left him."

I looked down at the bruises like they weren't even mine. That voice in my head—the one that sounded like a scolded little girl—whispered, *You should be ashamed. You knew better. You came back anyway.*

Liz looked at me. "Girl, you are an abused woman. You need to get out of there before he hurts you worse or kills you. You need to tell your counselor you're living with him again."

That was great advice, I thought. I would tell another woman the same thing: *if the guy isn't treating you well, it is time to leave.*

But there were days when Frank treated me like a queen, so it must have been something I was doing wrong.

Besides, it had been almost three months since I moved back in with Frank—I couldn't tell my counselor the truth now.

I didn't have the energy to talk anymore, nor did I even care, so I said, "I know—I'm working on a plan, I promise."

I was supposed to go see Judy, but I cancelled. I was still too ashamed that I was lying to her and everyone else.

The salon door creaked open. "Hey, is Chrissy here?"

My stomach dropped. Liz shot me a look, but I couldn't meet her eyes. I was already tucking my sleeves down, smoothing my hair, preparing the lie.

That shameful little girl inside me?

She didn't need to be told to stay silent. She already knew the script.

# Chapter 13

## The Devil Changes You

I was dancing with the devil. And I didn't even realize I'd already handed over my soul.

I didn't have a plan. I wasn't trying to be dramatic or reckless. I was just trying to survive each day without collapsing under the weight of it all.

Journaling has always been my escape from life. It serves as a therapeutic outlet, a sacred space where I can pour out my soul, confront my negative feelings, and connect with the deeper layers of my inner self. Writing allows me to process my experiences and emotions, turning chaos into clarity.

My love for words started in the silence between slammed doors and heavy sighs. In middle school, I bought those black Oxford Composition Notebooks and filled them with everything—daily dramas, secret heartbreaks, and dreams too fragile to say out loud.

My journal was my confessional, my sanctuary. The one place where I didn't have to smile, hide, or pretend.

However, one cold fall night changed everything. A chill was in the air and the firelight cast flickering shadows. Frank snatched the journal from my hands.

"Let's see what Chrissy's been writing about," he smirked.

I froze. That notebook held *everything*.

He read aloud, mocking my pain, twisting my words. "You're a terrible writer. Seriously, Chrissy—who's Shawn? You confide in him, but not me?"

Then, without hesitation, he whipped open the woodstove door, and flames engulfed my soul.

I watched the words turn to ashes.

A lifetime of secrets. Gone.

And when I finally broke down, he pulled it from the flames—too late—and said, "Oh, Chrissy. I'm so sorry." As his boots smashed out the fire.

A few days later, Frank brought me a new journal and said, "Maybe I haven't been emotionally available like you need."

He handed me the journal.

"Leave it out where I can read it!"

That night, I wrote my truth—uncensored. What follows was never meant to be read aloud:

Hey, maybe in the next life, I'll get it right. who knows? I sure didn't do this one right. My expectations were too high for almost everyone's definition of me. I pushed people too much; heck, both of my exes just told me, "You have a way of beating me down. Your expectations are unrealistic. I'm done." My children really don't talk to me. My own mother is disgusted by me, yet visits her convict daughter in jail. How ironic she only degrades me on how much of a bitch I am and how "oh well, that is how she is."

Can no one see my pain? No one reaches for me, yet I reach and reach for people. Do I feel too much and expect too much of this humankind? or am I just so unhappy with myself that everyone else sees me as a monster?

Funny, I guess I'll never know!

The pain that I feel sometimes is more than I can bear.

Sometimes, it isn't easy to breathe, and I just want to have it all end. But they say taking your own life is selfish. Really do the other people feel your pain? Do they call you? are they concerned with your emotional well-being? No, and why? because we are all so busy, we just worry about own fucking feelings. Oh, I know, call me a self, self-centered bitch! Really, it is all okay to call me this! It really is because maybe that is all I am in the end...when I am gone, I'm more than sure more gross things will come out of their mouth about how crazy I "was!"

Crazy, yes, crazy for a life of fun! It's crazy to live and see things "differently" than how most people see things.

And

maybe

just a dreamer......

or

Someone who just wanted to be noticed, just once, to be someone to someone! But then they say if you don't love yourself, you can never love anyone else.

Well... When your own mother is disgusted by you, your own children view you as a waste of space in life, and every man you have ever loved does not know how simple it is to love me.

Inflexible

contrary

difficult

a bitch

an asshole

a slut, lol

Let us, by all means, not forget what everyone says about me a given day:

CRAZY

Well, let me not disappoint you all and show you how right you all are...everyone is so much superior to me and so much smarter than stupid me.

There are positive things about Christina Gail Martin. She can make almost anyone laugh, even if it means at her own expense.

credit of edit by the superior F of Tannersville, PA

When I woke up, Frank had signed the note.

"Edited by the Superior F of Tannersville, PA."

My pain had become a punchline.

I headed down the stairs, dreading the day. Frank was drinking coffee at the kitchen table. I heard him on the phone with his cousin. "I'm worried about her; I think she's losing her grip on reality. I'm scared she might try to kill herself or me."

I confronted Frank about the conversation, and he screamed, "Why are you spying on me?"

He stood up, walked into the kitchen, and came back holding a cup of coffee. Calm, almost casual. He gestured for me to sit down.

"Chrissy," he said, voice steady but heavy with accusation, "I had no idea just how mentally ill you were. I love you, but I'm scared. I think you might try to hurt yourself—or me."

I froze.

"I don't think your therapist is helping you. Honestly... you're getting worse, not better."

He knew my history. He knew I married my first husband a month after high school graduation, with a three-month-old baby on my hip. We were both too young, too lost, and wildly unprepared for the life we were trying to build.

The first time I found out he cheated, my world cracked open. I was 28 with three little kids and a heart full of pain. My husband and my children were everything. When he betrayed me, I felt shattered—abandoned in a storm of fear and confusion. That night, I downed a bottle of vodka and a bottle of sleeping pills. I didn't want to die. I just wanted the pain to stop. It was a desperate cry for someone—anyone—to see me, to help me.

Right after I swallowed the pills, I called my mother-in-law. The ambulance came. I survived.

After that, I threw myself into therapy, into healing. I grew up fast. But some wounds run deeper than any therapist's office can reach. I slapped a Band-Aid over mine, hoping it would hold, but the infection never left. It festered beneath the surface, waiting.

When Frank told me we needed to see a counselor, something old and raw stirred inside me. It wasn't just his words—it was the way he looked at me. Like I was broken beyond repair.

The shame hit first. Then the guilt.

All the things I'd buried—the lies, the trauma, the choices I regretted—came flooding back like a wave I couldn't stop. I broke down, sobbing uncontrollably, my body shaking with the weight of it all.

"You're a mess," Frank said coldly. "No one could possibly love you like this. Chrissy, get yourself under control."

Then he handed me a glass of wine.

"Drink this. It'll calm you down."

I took it like a shot. My hands trembled as I grabbed the bottle and poured more. I hadn't eaten. The wine burned through me fast, numbing everything.

That's when he looked me in the eyes and said it.

"Maybe you should've died when you tried to kill yourself all those years ago. Maybe you are dead—and this is Hell. You just keep repeating your life, making the same bad choices over and over and over again."

His words didn't just hurt—they pierced.

And somewhere in the back of my mind, I wondered... was he right?

I screamed, "I'm not crazy—you are driving me insane!"

He shoved me outside. Barefoot. No coat.

The door slammed. I punched the glass in rage and desperation. My hand broke through the window. I didn't even feel it.

"You're crazy," he hissed, opening the door. "Maybe you should just kill yourself for good this time."

Frank walked past me and said, "Chrissy, you scare me. Do the world a favor and down some more pills, and stop torturing your family and me."

I stood there with blood dripping from the cuts on my hand, and the next thing I knew, I was in the bathroom, popping one Benadryl pill after another, when Frank came back into the house and found me.

He started to scream at me, "What the fuck are you doing?" He grabbed the bottle and asked how many I had taken. I had no idea; it was a small bottle, not enough to kill me. I had grabbed the bottle of wine when I ran up the stairs and took another huge gulp.

Frank stuffed his finger down my throat, trying to get me to throw up, and said, "Jesus Christ, Chrissy, what am I going to do with you? I knew something like this would happen. I can't live this way anymore. You are too much of a risk."

It is all a blur at this point, but Frank put me in the car and raced to the hospital. I remember him being followed by a police car, and when we pulled up to the emergency entrance and he got out of the car, a cop pulled a gun on him because he was speeding and didn't pull over.

Frank said, "I need a wheelchair. My girlfriend just tried to kill herself."

Someone came out of the ER and put me in a wheelchair. They took me into a room and started to ask me questions. I watched as the cop took Frank into another room.

"Oh my God, she's covered in bruises." I heard one of the nurses say.

I wanted to disappear.

Someone asked if Frank had hit me. I couldn't answer. My throat closed. My eyes welled up. The shame—thick and choking—climbed up my chest.

A nurse left the room. I watched her whisper to a police officer. They looked at me like I was a puzzle they already knew how to solve.

I must have passed out. The next day, I woke up, and they moved me into another room, and I talked to someone on a monitor.

I lied and told her I was leaving him. I told her I was seeing a counselor and that I needed to get home. I had to get my dog and work the next day, or I would be fired, and then I would be stuck with Frank forever.

I must have put on one hell of a show for the therapist because they let me leave the hospital.

I didn't have my cell phone, and the only number I could remember was my mom's.

She showed up at the hospital, looked at me, and said, "What are you doing?"

I had blood all over my pants where I had cut my hand when I punched the glass on the back door. My mascara was running down my face.

The entire car ride back to Frank's place, she just lectured me on how I was ruining my life and that I needed to get my shit together.

She said, "Do I need to come to his house and shoot him for you to leave?"

All I heard was, "You're such an embarrassment."

Frank wasn't home.

I sat barefoot on the back steps, blood drying on my hands, mascara streaking down my face, watching chickens peck at the grass like nothing had happened.

No phone. No coat. No plan. No Daizy.

Just me. Still here.

And somehow, still hoping someone might come back for me.

That was my last cry for help.

And no one heard it.

Or no one cared.

You have to let everything fall apart
before you find out what's indestructible
about you. — Glennon Doyle Melton

# Chapter 14

## Chasing My Tail

Frank came home, looked up at the porch, and strolled towards me. He didn't say a word, and I felt a wave of fear wash over me as I thought, *Maybe he's done with me and won't let me back in.*

He put out his hand and said, "Oh, my poor Chrissy. Are you okay?"

I fell into his arms, sobbing. My broken soul melted into his dark, evil world.

I took a shower while Frank prepared breakfast for me. My favorite was a vegetable omelet with fried sweet potatoes, peppers, onions, and a slice of toast.

As I sat there sipping my coffee and eating, Frank said, "Chrissy, please, I need you to see a therapist. I'm really afraid for you. You might hurt yourself again or me."

I was exhausted. I agreed.

Frank offered to pay for my sessions, which I thought was strange since I had insurance.

He called around, and there was a place that a friend of his suggested. We made an appointment.

He said, "I know you're scared, but this is best for our relationship."

We went to the appointment, and Frank did most of the talking. He told the counselor that I didn't have any friends and that my own family did not talk to me anymore. He told the counselor how I lay around the house most days crying, drinking wine, and barely eating anything anymore.

"I've noticed she doesn't sleep much. She has stopped doing all the things she used to love, like painting and working out every day. She just stopped."

The counselor looked at me and asked, "Is that true?"

I stared at the counselor for a bit and said, "He doesn't like my friends or my family, so I can't invite them over. I don't eat because he told me I'm fat. I stopped painting because he told me I was a terrible painter."

I started to cry, and Frank said, "I just don't understand her anymore. I offered to have her friends and family over for dinner, but she said she was just too tired. She said her mom doesn't care about her, just her sister."

Then he took my hand and said, "Baby, didn't I pay for you to take painting classes, but you just stopped going?"

I looked at him and said, "You are lying. Why are you saying all these lies? That is not what happened."

In a slow and calm voice, Frank just sat there and stated, "Oh, Chrissy, I'm so sorry you feel this way. Did I not offer you to come here to work on our relationship?"

I stood up and yelled, "You are lying!"

The counselor asked me to leave the room and wait downstairs because he needed to talk to Frank alone.

I walked out of the office, straight down the stairs, and flopped onto a chair. The secretary came out to check that I hadn't left and to offer me a glass of water. I was so numb; I didn't question why the counselor wanted to talk to Frank alone. I just thought, *Wasn't this my appointment?*

When Frank came out, the counselor told me to make another appointment for next week alone.

I made the appointment.

Frank and I went home; he looked at me and said, "That was a test. I wanted to see if you would tell the truth—tell the counselor that you tried to kill yourself."

Frank continued, "But, no, Chrissy lied and turned it all on Frank. Frank is a bad person. Frank is a monster. Poor Chrissy is the victim."

"Don't worry. I told the counselor what you did, and I stopped at your grandmother's while you were in the hospital and told her."

I couldn't believe what he was telling me. Was I the bad person? Was I playing a victim?

The next day, I called and canceled my appointment. I didn't tell Frank. I was afraid to go back. Maybe Frank would have them lock me up.

I snuck around the house, spying on him whenever he was on the phone or friends came over. He was always talking about how sick I was in the head.

I came downstairs as he and the neighbor next door were talking. I heard him say, "Oh, Lynn, I'm so worried about her. She looks terrible, and I'm so afraid she's going to kill me one day."

Lynn said, "I'm worried about her too. She's always making up stories about how awful you treat her. Please call us if you need anything, and we'll pray she gets better."

I felt hurt and overwhelmed as I stood there listening to their conversation. The thought of facing anyone was too much to bear. I shared secrets about Frank and me with Lynne. I believed I could trust her, but now I realized I couldn't trust anyone.

His cousin was supposed to come for a visit and stay with us, but I heard Frank tell him on the phone, "I'm so sorry, but now is not a good time to visit. Chrissy's emotionally a wreck right now. I can't leave her alone for one second. I'm terrified for my life."

By the holidays, I wanted nothing to do with anyone. It took all my energy to just get up and go to work. Who could I trust?

I made excuse after excuse for not being able to go anywhere. The neighbors invited us for Christmas dinner, but I told Frank I wasn't feeling well. I could not bear to see Lynne, knowing she thought so poorly of me. Frank went without me.

Most days, I sat around the house crying. It seemed my only escape was going to work. I was free from Frank.

Frank would frequently tell me he would stop by to see me, but to my relief, he never once came.

I lied to most people at work and told them I wasn't with Frank anymore. Shawn, Beth, and Dave were about the only people I talked to still. It was nice to pretend that my life was perfect when I was at work.

But I soon fucked that up as well.

Frank hated it when I quoted him.

We had a heated discussion, and I quoted one of Frank's emails, "Go and Love Again."

Frank burst out laughing. "That is the dumbest platitude. What are you going to do? Go love again as shitty as you have in the past?" He got right in my face and screamed, "You probably pushed your first husband to cheat on you! No man could ever love you!"

I punched the wall.

Not out of rage—out of pure, unfiltered frustration.

The drywall cracked. My hand didn't.

It shattered.

And in that instant, everything else around me did too.

Frank screamed from the other room, "Don't come in here. I have a gun beside me—you scare me, Chrissy."

I cradled my busted hand and collapsed onto the couch.

The pain was white-hot, but the real pain was deeper.

The pain of disappearing.

Of becoming the girl who tiptoed around a man who called her crazy, then told everyone else he feared for his life.

That night, I slept on the couch and prayed my hand was not broken, but I knew it was. The amount of anger that festered inside me exploded, and the force of my hand hitting the plaster wall crushed two knuckles and snapped a bone.

I lay on the couch, held ice on my hand, and thought. *He told me I pick on him, mistreat him, belittle him, and talk poorly to him. This is his house, not mine. If I don't like his rules, I can leave.*

I barely slept with the throbbing of my hand.

I woke up on the couch. I knew it was broken and needed to go to the emergency department. I sat up and said, "What am I doing?"

Frank came downstairs, and I told him I needed to get my hand looked at.

"I'm not driving you to the ER. Remember what happened last time. I'm not having a gun pointed at me again and people thinking I beat you." He started to walk away. "You did this to yourself. You messed up big time, and you can fix it on your own. I have shit to do today."

My hand was swollen three times its normal size, and the pain was nearly as excruciating as the numbness within my heart and mind.

I'm right-handed, so driving with my left hand was a challenge.

Luck was on my side. We had gotten a snowstorm the night before.

I lied to the ER nurse; I told him I slipped on the ice going to my car.

The nurse said they needed to take an X-ray, and just like that, the mood shifted—everything suddenly felt heavier.

As I sat in the hospital waiting for the nurse to return, I thought, *Chrissy, you did good this time.*

I had tiny, pretty little hands, but not anymore. My right hand has this HUGE, ugly lump where I used to have a pinky knuckle and a pinky that does not work anymore. NOTE to self: "Anger gets you NOWHERE BUT causes scars and pain for the rest of your life."

They set me up with an orthopedic doctor right away. The bone needed to be reset.

The office was right around the corner, and they could see me immediately. I sat in the exam room, waiting. When the doctor who worked in my unit came through the door. Again, out of shame, I lied. "I slipped on the ice."

He told me, "You will need to set up surgery immediately. I need to reset the bone and put a pin through your little finger and scrape out the bone fragments in your knuckles." Looking at my hand, he said, "I'm not sure how well I can reconstruct your two last knuckles, but I will do my best.

"You will be out of work for three months."

I looked at him and pleaded, "Isn't there anything else you can do for a quick fix?"

I was always looking for a quick fix. *Oh, Chrissy, I don't think there is a "quick fix" to this one girl!*

The doctor said, "Have you eaten today?"

"No."

"I can reset the bone here in the office and put a soft cast on it. It will hurt like Hell, but I know you, and you're strong; you can handle the pain."

He went out and gathered supplies and a nurse.

Resetting the bone hurt ten times worse than the pain I was in, but it was a "quick fix."

*I am a bad girl anyway, lying to everyone. I need to be punished.*

The doctor informed me that I would wear the soft cast and come in for weekly X-rays to ensure the bone did not move and was healing. I would be out of work for about two months and need physical therapy after the bone healed to regain full use of my little finger.

Another day that was a blur. I left the office with an appointment for the following week. I sat in my car and didn't even have the energy to cry. I looked down at my hand, throbbing in pain, wrapped in a plastic cast, and thought, *What the fuck did you do now?*

I received a few text messages from Frank, so I placed my phone between my legs on the seat of my car and used my left hand to call him to tell him I had broken my hand and would be home soon. He said, "Drive safe, see you soon."

How did this all happen? When would the craziness stop?

I called my mom. She said, "Do you need me to come get you and drive you home?"

I told her, "No! I'm fine. I can drive myself."

She told me to keep her updated and let her know if I needed anything.

I hung up with my mom, my fingers trembling against the cold plastic cast.

I wanted to say:

**Yes.**

I need someone to save me.

From Frank.

From this nightmare.

From myself.

But I didn't say it because I knew the truth.

No one was coming.

This was my mess. My storm.

And I had to crawl my way out—alone.

I sat in silence and stared at my hand. This ugly, disfigured hand. A permanent reminder of how deep I had sunk. Of how long I'd been chasing my tail—running in frantic circles inside someone else's cage, begging for love, bleeding for scraps.

It wasn't just my hand that was broken.

It was me.

And maybe—just maybe—that meant it was time to start putting myself back together.

*But how the fuck do I do that?*

*Where do I begin?*

# Chapter 15

## Planning The Escape

The cold steel of a handgun pressed against my temple.

I didn't scream. I didn't flinch.

I just opened my eyes and I stared him straight in the eyes.

I knew I would carry the shame of that day forever.

Not just for breaking my arm—but for breaking my promise to myself.

I let fear win. Again.

When I got home, Frank said, "You have this endless ability to give to everyone else, but I think it's your downfall."

*Why am I always doing my best to make sure everyone else is happy?*

I called Judy, my counselor, and canceled my appointment that week. I felt too ashamed to tell her what had happened. And how was I going to explain my broken arm?

I depended on Frank for even the littlest things, like washing my hair, spreading butter on toast, and opening a carton of almond milk.

Frank refused to drive me to my weekly appointments.

I had learned to shut up and not push him.

The fighting stopped, and we spent our evenings watching TV and enjoying the warmth of the fireplace. I loved the Netflix series *Penny Dreadful* and entertained Frank by watching *Dexter* at least once a week.

One night, I had offered to watch *Maleficent* or *Avatar*, but Frank mocked the movies I liked—anything whimsical he dismissed as stupid. I stopped suggesting them.

Frank said, "We can watch *At Play in the Fields of the Lord*. It's a 1991 movie about a lost indigenous tribe destroyed by man's greed. Or better yet, since you like quoting my emails. Let's watch *Harold and Maude*."

A few days later, we were upstairs discussing what I would do once my hand was fully recovered. I mentioned maybe we could take a trip to Puerto Rico— when, out of nowhere, Frank grabbed me by the neck and slammed me against the doorway.

I hit my head, and he pushed me back.

I heard Frank walk down the hallway into our bedroom; when he came out, he was screaming and waving a gun in my face, "Get the fuck out of my house, get the fuck out, get the fuck out."

As if time stopped, I stood in the doorway to the bathroom—frozen, and Frank pressed the gun against my temple. As I felt the cold steel of a handgun gouging into my head, and his hot, stale coffee breath on my face.

I didn't scream.

I didn't flinch.

I glared straight into his eyes and said, "Go ahead— shoot me."

It felt as though I was standing up for myself. For the first time in my life, I was regaining control of my own life.

Frank pushed with all his strength. I hit the doorway frame and fell to my knees.

He turned and walked down the stairs screaming, "Get the fuck out of my house, get the fuck out, get the fuck out."

I picked up Daizy and walked down the stairs. I grabbed my purse and headed for the back door. Frank said, "There you go, walking out on me again."

I dropped to my knees and just bawled like a baby.

Something inside of me died that day.

And something else…. finally woke up.

Frank said, "Oh my Chrissy, what am I going to do with you. You are such a mess." He pulled me up and just held onto me.

Then Frank's landline rang—as if the Universe had heard me and said, 'It's time."

It was one of his tenants—they were moving out.

Frank said, "Chrissy, I'll be gone all day for a few weeks. I've got to gut this apartment completely." It was the break I needed.

I received a phone call from HR at work, and my short-term disability would run out on March 7th.

I had to move fast. Although I was supposed to be in therapy for my hand, I needed to concentrate on planning my escape. I called Judy and made a new appointment. I had to tell her the truth.

When I walked into Judy's office, she asked me what had happened to my hand and why I had canceled my appointments the last few weeks. I sat down and told her everything.

She looked at me. "I had a hunch you were still with him. It is not easy to leave a toxic relationship as quickly as you did without going back. I had it on my calendar to call you today if you didn't show up or if you canceled again."

I just stared at the floor—*she saw through my lies the whole time.*

"Chrissy, you did nothing wrong," she said gently. "The shame you feel is from years of abuse and lying to yourself and others.

"It's called Complex Post-Traumatic Stress Disorder. With therapy, you can break the cycle, create new habits, and learn to love yourself for who you are."

She leaned forward. "But right now, we need to get you to safety. Do you have a plan?"

I told her how I was moving my things into storage and looking for a new job out of state.

"Don't you have someplace safe? You can call the police to get your things out."

I told her that at this point, I was accustomed to his verbal threats and knew how to appease his ego to maintain peace.

"Chrissy, do you know why you thrive so well as a nurse?"

"Not really. I just figured I was an adrenaline junkie."

"Being exposed to abuse has changed your brain. With PTSD, we have known for a long time that when someone is repeatedly subjected to traumatic experiences, their frontal cortex of the brain changes, significantly shrinking. But new research points out that these same people thrive in otherwise highly stressful situations, such as your job as a nurse. You can handle life-threatening situations and remain calm in stressful situations, saving lives."

"Oh, wow! That's a good thing, right?"

"Yes, and no; you've learned how to thrive in chaos because your brain learned to survive there. But now, we have to teach it peace."

"Yeah, I tend to jump in with both feet before looking.... Oh, wait. I lack the fear factor for danger because of the changes in my brain."

Judy nodded, "Yes, that is correct. Now I need you to promise me that you will leave when you notice that the situation at Frank's is escalating."

I promised.

Judy's words stayed with me: "Your whole life trained you for this kind of chaos."

I started to wonder... Where did that training begin?

I thought about my mom. She was born into poverty. Her dad was a cook, and they moved from town to town as he searched for work. My maternal grandmother was very outspoken, drank, smoked, and swore.

When my grandmother was angry at someone, she spoke of them as if they were dead—even if it was family. She disowned anyone she was angry at.

My mom shared stories of how her parents would pack her and her sister in the middle of the night to avoid getting evicted from their apartment. She recounted wearing shoes that were too small, which hurt her feet, and how her clothes were also too tight, leading to other kids at school making fun of her. However, no school she attended lasted long due to their frequent moves; she went to thirteen different schools while growing up.

The person I knew my mom to be was a people pleaser. She would do anything for anyone, but there was a price to pay.

She lent people money but would then say, "I was supposed to go on vacation this year, but I lent you money, so now I can't go."

They would offer to pay her back, but she would say, "Oh, no worries—pay me back whenever you can. It's fine. I'll just go on vacation another year. It's not like I'd been planning this trip for months."

My mom put all her dreams on hold to keep our family together. She knew my dad had been cheating on her for years, but she never had a family while growing up and turned a blind eye to his actions.

I'm sure she was unhappy in her marriage because all she did was complain and nag my dad for everything he did wrong or for the things he didn't do.

I once asked my dad why he waited until my younger sister moved out to file for divorce. He told me, "What kind of life would you girls have if I left you alone with your mother?"

Everyone in my family seemed to play it safe and stay in their own homemade version of Hell, slowly dying.

My life had been influenced by so many people who stayed in their comfort zone, never chased their dreams, and were *afraid of failing, scared to live.*

After my session with Judy I was so overwhelmed with thoughts. I needed to talk to someone.

I called Beth. She said, "Do you need a place to stay? You know you are always welcome here anytime."

"No. I have a plan. I got myself into this mess, and I'm gonna get myself out."

"I love you, Sis. I'm here if you need anything."

I knew she was—she was always there for me thick or thin.

Monday through Friday, when Frank left the house, I packed and moved boxes to the top of the garage, where Frank never went.

*Here you are, packing up again and leaving yet another man. It's just another mess.*

Frank had some of his mom's belongings in the top of the garage, so I placed a few of those items where I had taken my things, filling the emptiness so he wouldn't notice.

I began searching for jobs in another state to make it more difficult for Frank to locate me. On the weekends, I tiptoed around, doing my best to keep my big mouth shut and maintain peace within the confines of "His" home.

I discovered a job in my specialty with a large sign-on bonus, and the hospital even offered to cover my moving expenses. I applied, and within a few days, I received a call from Human Resources. The HR representative arranged a phone interview with the unit director. Who said, "I'm highly impressed with your experience, and if you're interested, I'll take the next steps."

They wanted to conduct an in-person interview and would cover all expenses: my flight, hotel, food, and even provide transportation from the airport to the hotel. I told Frank, "Hey, I think we might need to take a short break from each other. I could do a three-month travel assignment, and then we could reassess where we stand at the end of my contract."

"You know what?" Frank said, "That sounds perfect."

I had to sneak out and rent a U-Haul truck with a car carrier. Then I made plans with my son to fly him from Florida to Pennsylvania and drive with him across the country to Oregon.

To freedom I thought.

During the day, when Frank was gone, I searched online for apartments and found an adorable white two-bedroom house less than a mile from the hospital. I was set to move in on April 1st—my birthday!

I rented a storage unit down the street and began moving boxes there. I spent my days packing and transporting boxes.

Every box I packed was a silent rebellion.

Every lie I told him was a breadcrumb back to myself.

My body shook with anxiety, but my soul was already halfway to Oregon.

I had one issue: the neighbors. While moving boxes into the garage, I told Lynn that I was decluttering and relocating things. But now, what would I say as I carried the boxes from the garage to my car?

She must have sensed something was off because she came out the back door and asked me, "Are you finally leaving him?"

I looked at her and replied, "Yes, please don't tell him."

She smiled and said, "Let me help you." She grabbed a box and began loading it into my car.

I lied when I told Frank I had found a job not too far away. I told him it was in Virginia, but they needed me to come in for an interview, "I'll be doing all the paperwork and training for a few days." He knew nothing about travel nursing, so I knew I could tell him this. I told him I knew he was busy, so I would get my mom to watch the dog.

I packed a small bag, and Frank drove my doggie and me to my mom's house. He walked me to the door, and when my mom saw him, she said, "You can get off my porch; you are not welcome here."

"I love you, Chrissy. Be safe," he said, not realizing I was finally doing exactly that—keeping myself safe. From him.

When he pulled away, I cried. I stayed at my mom's that night, and she drove me to the airport in the morning. It was March 21, just over a year since I had moved in with Frank.

One whole year.

Vanished.

Swallowed by silence and shadow.

Twelve months of slow unraveling—of watching my dreams decay, my light dim, my spirit hollow out.

It's haunting how much a single year can take from you.

How time, once filled with promise, can turn into a graveyard of what could have been.

It was the second time in my life I had flown alone, and I was terrified.

I sat on the plane, watching the world grow smaller beneath me. 2,795 miles between me and the man I used to love.

Between who I was and who I was becoming.

This wasn't just a flight.

It was an escape. A rebirth.

A whispered promise to the girl I used to be:

*We're going to be okay now. Just breathe, Chrissy. Breathe.*

There will be countless moments in your life
when you are asked to lose yourself or lose
someone else. Choose wisely. — Unknown

# Chapter 16

## Dancing With Demons

It felt like a door had finally opened. The interview went better than I imagined—they loved me and wanted me to start in April. For the first time in a long time, I felt chosen.

I flew home and told Frank I would start my travel assignment in April. The next day, I went to my appointment with Judy and shared the great news with her. She said, "Getting away from this place and starting fresh is what you might need. But you must continue with your therapy to heal fully. Your wounds are deep, and hiding from them will not make them disappear."

I had one more orthopedic appointment, and when I arrived, the doctor said, "You haven't been to therapy at all. Why?"

I knew I had to start being honest—with everyone. I explained my living situation and that I needed him to clear me so I could start my new job.

He looked at me and said, "Chrissy, don't ever go back to him. I knew you were lying about your hand. Promise me you'll leave and never return."

"Oh, I'm never going back. My new job is in Oregon, and I'm out of here!"

But as Shawn once said, "The witch is real—doubt fills our minds."

I was starting to have second thoughts about leaving him. Frank was on his best behavior, and we were getting along.

I heard my grandmother saying, "Be a better wife, and he won't hit you."

Drama and chaos were all I knew. When life was stressful and my relationships were falling apart, I felt a warm, comforting embrace.

*What if I fail in my new job? What if I move and no one likes me?* The witch of doubt screamed in my ear— *You've never left this town – what business do you have in dreaming of escaping?*

With my job lined up and the doctor's warning ringing in my ears, I thought the hardest part was over.

But the universe had one more test for me—a spiritual reckoning I never saw coming.

Frank offered to give me a farewell sweat lodge to provide safety for my trip. "I know Virginia's not that far away, but a sweat lodge will clear your mind."

I was looking forward to an intensely hot lodge to prepare me for my next journey in life.

We prayed as we placed the stone people on the lodge altar, collected the water, and gave our thanks. We started the fire to heat the rocks for our lodge, and you looked at me and asked, "Do you want to do mushrooms and have a full experience today?"

I was shocked because he knew I was a nurse and could not do drugs. But he said, "Mushrooms are non-detectable and will fully unlock your mind."

*Maybe this is what I need to break the cycles of fear that have eroded patterns within my brain.* I asked, "Are you sure?"

He said, "Why not!"

After everything I had been through with Frank, why did I still believe that he had my best interests in mind?

Frank handed me the mushrooms and said, "Do you trust me?"

That was an odd question. "Yes, I trust you."

He said, "Most people don't like the taste of mushrooms; they think they're gross, and a lot of people throw up just trying to eat them."

I laughed, standing there eating them like candy. There was nothing at all gross in their taste. Why was this? Was I just so eager to find my answers? But I did not even know the questions I wanted to ask! I had become so lost over the last year and so depressed out of FEAR! But fear of what!

I ate the mushrooms—we went outside and started the ceremony. I prayed, "Please, Great Mystery, give me the questions so I can find the answers to make a leap. I call on my ancestors to show me what I am so afraid of."

The second lesson from the universe is *Be careful what you ask for.*

Soon, the effects of the hallucinogen took control of my mind, and my rose-colored glasses shattered. The truth was staring me straight in the face—I couldn't deny it any longer.

Sitting in the lawn chair, I felt my bare feet melting into the grass. I saw Frank transform from a human to a small hairy troll—an earth creature.

The creature said, "You are safe; I'm here to protect you."

The troll reached for my hand and said, "No, it's okay, come with me."

I looked at my hands, and they were changing into troll hands!

Frank's feet were like those of the goat man from *Narnia*, and I screamed, "NO! I'm not an earth creature; I'm not going!"

"Okay, it's time to get in the inipi."

I couldn't move.

The troll grabbed my shoulders and walked me to the inipi.

It had rained all day, and the earth was wet and covered in mud. The cold mud swished under my feet as I entered the lodge. I sat there frozen in fear, staring at the hole in the middle of the inipi.

Frank placed the first set of rocks in the tent, and I watched each rock morph into a human skull. The ground surrounding the hole turned black like charcoal. The blackness moved closer to me; the blanket I was sitting on started turning black, and then my arms and shirt were engulfed with a blackness I was sure was Hell itself.

I knew if I stayed there, I was going to die. I crawled to the door of the lodge and the troll was there. I looked at him and said, "I'm going to die. The stone people are dragging me down to Hell."

"Stay inside. You're fine."

I looked up at him, and he turned into the Devil.

I pushed him aside and screamed, "I have to get out of here."

I ran into the house.

I realized I had spent my whole life chasing chaos because peace felt unfamiliar.

I married young out of guilt. Stayed in a toxic marriage because I believed I deserved the pain. I destroyed the one relationship that was kind to me because I didn't think I was worthy of love.

I had no idea how to love myself—or even that I was allowed to.

That night, the darkness didn't just show me Frank's truth. It showed me mine.

I wasn't a prisoner of any man. I was a prisoner of my own shame.

And I was finally ready to break the chains.

I played in Hell that night.

But I made it out.

Barefoot, muddy, and reborn.

People tend to raise the child inside
of them rather than the child in
front of them — Joe Newman

# Chapter 17

## Boomerang Effects

I stood in that sewing store, invisible to my own mother, and realized I'd spent a lifetime dancing for people who refused to see me.

The next day, I had my last therapy appointment with Judy, and it wasn't far from my mom's work, so I stopped in to see her. She worked in a sewing store, and when I walked in one of the sales associates asked me if I needed help with anything. I said, "Oh, I'm here to see my mom."

"Who's your mom, sweetie? I think you might be in the wrong store."

My mom came out from around the corner, and I said, "Hi, Mom."

The woman said, "You have another daughter? You have only talked about Beth. I didn't know you had two daughters."

I immediately said, "Oh yeah, I'm the daughter with the college degree. Not the one who went to federal prison."

My mom said, "Shut the fuck up," and pushed me to the front door.

I looked at her and said, "Wow, so I don't even exist to you, do I?"

In that moment, I stopped being the daughter who waited to be chosen. I walked out knowing I'd never get the mother I needed—but I could become the woman I needed.

I told Judy about my experience with mushrooms. She told me how therapists were starting to use hallucinogens to treat depression and schizophrenia. "It's dangerous to do what you did without the proper training. Last night could have gone way worse. Please, do not ever do that again without consulting a specialist."

I promised her I wouldn't.

I then told her what happened with my mom and she asked me how that made me feel.

"Pissed off, but not surprised."

"Why not surprised?"

"I guess I figured with all the shit I put my parents through they kind of signed off on me. Besides maybe she blames me for her life not turning out the way she wanted it to. I mean she was in college to become a nurse when she got pregnant with me and had to drop out and marry my dad."

Judy said, "And why do you feel this way?"

"Well, what if I wasn't born? She would have had a totally different life. Maybe the one she wanted to have. She always talked about traveling and seeing the world. She didn't do that with my dad."

"Well, Chrissy, I'm sure she did the best she could to provide for you. And you know what, if she hadn't traveled and reached her goals, that is not your fault."

I just looked at Judy. "Oh my God, you are right. I always wanted to go to college and when I got the chance I did it."

Judy then said, "Okay, let's do some exercises and explore your past a bit deeper."

With prompts, I remembered how my youngest daughter was the spitting image of me when I was her age. She and her dad were arguing, and he grabbed her by the throat, and her feet were dangling off the floor.

In that instant, it was like watching a ghost from my past—a mirror reflecting back everything I had survived.

I was 14 when my husband started beating me. He would smash my head off concrete walls, slam my leg in the car door frame, and punch me in the face. I couldn't let history repeat itself. I had to stop this curse. I couldn't let this continue any longer.

I kicked my husband out of the house, packed a bag of his things, and set them on the porch. I went to the courthouse, filed a Protection from Abuse order, and breathed a sigh of relief when the police showed up at the door and served him the paperwork.

I stayed in that first marriage because shame shackled me to a role I never auditioned for. "Be a better wife," they said—so I played the part until it nearly killed me.

We had been together since I was fourteen, and the chaos of the toxic relationship was all I knew. So I took him back.

Then things changed when I received a phone call: my dad was dead.

My dad had high blood pressure, and they said that he had an aneurysm that burst in his neck. I was angry that my dad had died. I didn't want to attend his funeral, but my mom forced me. I didn't visit his grave; I couldn't bear the thought of him being gone.

I was working part-time as a camp secretary and planning a baby shower for our oldest. I sat in my dining room, *What am I doing with my life?*

I met May, a nurse working at the camp. We exchanged phone numbers, and after camp ended, she invited me to visit her in Washington State. She said, "You should become a nurse. You'll make good money."

I spent months screaming to God, *Why did you take my dad away?*

I never had a good relationship with my dad. Yet, I felt like a little girl who needed her daddy after he died. There were so many things I wanted him to do—be there for me, protect me, just tell me once that he loved me and was proud of me.

But he never did, and now I would never hear the words I desperately wanted to hear—"Chrissy, I'm proud of how you turned out, and I love you."

Judy asked me, "What upsets you the most about your dad's passing? You said you wanted him to tell you how proud he was of you. What did you want to hear?"

"I think I just wanted to say sorry for being a pain in the ass. I wanted him to see that I'd changed—that I wasn't the same broken girl anymore."

"What is one thing you did that was positive after your dad passed?"

"Oh, that's easy to answer."

My dad passed in August, and I had never taken a trip by myself anywhere, let alone get on a plane by myself. May, the nurse I met at the camp, said, "Why don't you come to see me and clear your mind?"

I bought a ticket to Washington and spent two weeks clearing the fog from my head and asking myself what I wanted to do with my life.

When I got home, I drove straight to our local community college and took the placement test. The weirdest thing was that after I finished taking it, the receptionist came out and said, "You know you took this test ten years ago."

Judy asked, "How did that make you feel?"

"Upset, ashamed of myself for giving up on my dreams."

When my youngest daughter started school, it seemed the perfect time for me to take college classes. I took the placement test, did my financial aid, and found out I would be going for free and receiving a Pell Grant. I signed up for evening classes and bought my books. But the day I was supposed to start, my husband called to tell me he would be working late—he never worked late!

Between being called a failure my whole life, having my husband tell me I couldn't do anything without him, and having little support and minimal to zero self-confidence, I didn't call and ask if my mom could watch my kids. No, instead, I blamed my husband for my being unable to go.

Ten years later, I knew I had to show my kids a better life. That anything was possible. I had a granddaughter now—nothing would hold me back. Besides, I had to prove to my dad I was worth something. I was more than a troublemaker. More than just a stupid, loud-mouthed kid! And I thought my mom would be proud of me for pursuing the degree she wanted.

January 2007. Three classes, books on a credit card, and hope pinned to a Pell Grant.

College was exciting and new to me, but it also made me realize that my life was a mess.

Soon, I recognized that I was holding myself back and that I could, indeed, live my life without my husband.

I spent three years fighting for a divorce. I tried to sell our house, but he refused to sign the paperwork every time I found a buyer. I ultimately filed for bankruptcy and lost my house.

During college, I met a man who held two bachelor's degrees and a graduate degree and was a professor, and he changed my world. We dated while I completed my nursing degree and then got married. Our entire relationship lasted six years. I kept the house; I would not lose another one!

I had been divorced for only four months when I met Frank, and I was not ready for another relationship.

Judy said, "This is good. You are seeing the cycle of abuse in your life. The first step is acknowledging what is happening. The second step is getting out of the toxic relationship. It is not easy to leave."

I knew I had to leave. I needed to confront my deepest fears and prove that I was not a failure—that I could escape this small town and break free from my chains.

Leaving Frank didn't mean I gave up on him like all the other women. It meant I was stronger than the poison, and it was not my responsibility to *save* him—I had to save myself.

# Chapter 18

## Falling Fast

Leaving wasn't the hard part. *Staying gone*—that was the war.

My son, Jack, flew up from Florida, and I met him to grab the U-Haul truck. When Mom, my son, and I arrived at Frank's, he walked out the back door, got in his car, and left.

My mom looked around and said, "Good. Let's get you out of this hellhole before it swallows you whole."

We took a mattress and bed frame that Frank and I had bought. We also packed up a dresser that I had repainted from one of Frank's units, which a tenant had left behind.

I turned around and looked at all the things I was leaving behind. Not just furniture—*parts of myself.* My antique dressers, my desk stacked with years of journals, the books that saw me through every storm, even the pheasant my dad had shot and had mounted—*gone*. If I took them, Frank would know. And if Frank knew, none of us would be safe.

I ran out the front door, and we drove off to the storage unit.

I had rented an 8-by-10-foot unit filled with my belongings, which I had spent months secretly packing and moving.

When I opened the unit, my mom said, "I see now why you got the larger U-Haul truck."

After we packed the contents of the storage unit in the back of the U-Haul, my mom and son dropped me off at the house to grab my car and meet them at a nearby diner.

When we pulled up, Frank's car was sitting in the driveway. My mom said, "I'll go in with you to get the dog."

I said, "No, Mom. I'm okay. I'll meet you guys in a little while."

I went into the house to tell him goodbye. He was upstairs in the spare room. I asked him, "Why are you in here?"

His eyes were all bloodshot; I didn't know if it was from the stress of another woman leaving him or if he had been crying.

"I will not be able to sleep in our room until you come back," he said.

His voice cracked, and for a split second, I saw the boy inside the man. The one who never healed. The one I kept trying to fix, even as he broke me.

*Don't fall for it, Chrissy.*

I grabbed his hand and lied, "Oh, Frank, I'll be back before you know it. You can always come and visit me. Wouldn't that be nice?"

He looked at me and said, "Yeah, by the way, I don't think I ever even asked what city you're going to be working in."

My phone rang, and it was my mom. I looked at Frank, lied again, and said, "Baby, I have to go. I'll call you when I get there. I'll text you the address, and we can plan for you to come out."

I ran downstairs, grabbed my doggie, and a few more essentials I'd hidden away. I hurried out the door. I got in the car and thought my heart would jump out of my chest from beating so fast.

I wasn't just walking away from a man. I was walking away from every lie I told myself to survive him.

I drove out of his driveway to never return, or so I thought.

As I drove away crying, I thought about my grandmother—how she had grown up in a different time.

She was wrong to tell me, "Be a better wife, and he won't hit."

But was I doing the right thing now? Should I stay? Would anyone ever love me for who I was—or was I just too difficult?

*Breathe, Chrissy, just breathe.*

You are not too much. You are not impossible.

You are finally free.

No more second chances. No more soft landings for men who break women and call it love.

I didn't look back. I just kept driving.

*Healing doesn't mean the damage never existed. It means the damage no longer controls your life. — Akshay Dubey*

# Chapter 19

## Tea And Truth

I called Judy's office and scheduled an emergency appointment for that afternoon. But first, I needed tea with my grammy—the way we always did when the world felt too heavy.

My grandmother made me a cup of tea, a tradition we've shared since I was a teenager. We sat on the porch, gazing at the horse barn. I thought of my dad's horse and the time he took me riding. Beyond the field was the family lake where we had a picnic every weekend during the summer. My first wedding reception took place on this family property. My daughter's baby shower was held down at the lake. *I have so many memories of this land. I've lived in this town my whole life. Am I really supposed to leave?*

My grandmother looked at me and said, "I knew he was no good for you. He treated you poorly, just like your first husband did."

"But, Gram," I said, swallowing back the lump in my throat, "you always told me to be a better wife—and he wouldn't hit me."

She stared out at the barn. "Maybe I said it wrong. I just wanted you to bend... I was so afraid you'd break. You reminded me of myself—wild and loud and full of fire. No one ever taught me how to carry that with softness."

She gazed up at me, paused, and said, "Do you remember when I came to visit you after you two first got married? I saw your black eye, and I took him for a walk?"

I said, "Yes. He never told me what you said to him."

"I told him to go for a walk whenever he got mad...That a man does not hit a woman and if he ever hit you again, he would be dealing with me."

We embraced and I could feel how frail she was getting with age. I said, "I'm leaving, but I will be back to visit you."

My grandmother said, "Don't you dare ever go back to him...He's trouble. I'm old. I'm sure this is the last time I will see you."

I grabbed her and said, "Gram, don't say that. You will live forever." I couldn't imagine a world without my Grammy in it.

She said, "I have outlived two husbands, one child, two brothers, and a sister. We all die. By the way, have you visited your dad's grave yet?"

Oh my God, my dad's grave. Why did everyone think closure lived in a patch of grass and a piece of carved stone? I wasn't ready.

I looked at the floor and said, "No, Gram, not yet."

I knew I had to visit my dad's grave. I had to say goodbye.

I drove to Judy's office for my appointment. I told her I was having second thoughts about leaving. I said, "Maybe I'm better and I can stay away this time. I don't think I can leave my grandmother."

I told Judy about what my grandmother said.

"You will have second thoughts, third, fourth, and fifth thoughts. You'll leave. You might go back. You'll probably talk to him again. That's normal. It doesn't mean you've failed—it means you're healing in real time."

"Yes, I know. I've already spent thousands of dollars, and I've been preparing for this day for years. All I've ever wanted to do was get out of this small town and see the world."

"Exactly. When are you going to visit your dad's grave?"

*I'm not ready.* "I don't know yet."

"Chrissy, you will know when the right time is here. You will forgive him, and you will fully heal. Here is the name of an amazing friend of mine who recently moved to Oregon. I told her a little about you and that you would be in touch with her."

I said, "Thank you, I will call her and make an appointment. But you are wrong. I will never talk to him again, and I will most *definitely* never go back to him."

"Chrissy, leaving a toxic relationship is hard. You went back once, so the chances of you staying away are not in your favor. I hope and pray you are right and I am wrong. Please make sure you keep in touch and call my friend...Oh, I bought you a book to read.

She handed me the book *POWER: Surviving and Thriving After Narcissistic Abuse, Your Brain on Love Sex.* "The author is Shahida Arabi. She has several other books you can read, but I recommend starting with this one."

She handed me the *NLP Workbook* by Joseph O'Connor. "Then start working through this workbook. It's about Neurolinguistic Programming, and it will help you see the world more clearly and understand yourself and others better...Oh, how do you feel about your relationship with your mom?"

"Better, I'm learning to see things from the other person's viewpoint. I may not be the daughter she wanted me to be, or maybe I am and she just has a hard time expressing her feelings. I mean my grandmother was one tough cookie. I can't imagine how difficult it was growing up with her as your mother. My friend Shawn told me about John Grey's Letter. I wrote one to my mom, and did the steps, and I even burnt them."

"Oh yes, I'm familiar with 'The Feeling Letter.' That is another positive step in the healing process."

As we hugged goodbye, I could feel it—the shift inside me.

*Damn girl, you're doing it.*

*Breathe, Chrissy. Breathe.*

This time, the air tasted like freedom.

I didn't know if I'd see my Grammy again. But I carried her words with me—not the ones that hurt, but the ones that finally set me free.

Sometimes the hardest part of the journey is believing you're worthy of the trip. — Glenn Beck

# Chapter 20

## Turning The Page

For years, I believed I was broken. If I could just be a better wife, maybe then I'd be worthy of love. But trauma doesn't disappear because you beg it to. It burrows deep. And it drags you under.

When Judy said the words—*PTSD. Complex PTSD*—something inside me clicked into place. Suddenly, the puzzle of my life started making sense. Why my body turned to ice during emotional warfare. Why I felt like a terrified little girl, shrinking, hiding, ashamed.

I had always been calm in chaos. I thrived in it. As a corrections nurse, I treated men straight from the streets—cuffed, bloodied, wild-eyed. Didn't blink. Didn't flinch.

I volunteered to care for the detox patients no one else wanted to touch. One man warned me he'd stab me if I missed his IV. I didn't flinch—I hit it on the first try. Then he reached into his backpack and pulled out a knife. "This was your lucky day," he said. They later found seven knives on him.

And still—I wasn't afraid.

For a long time, I wondered what was wrong with me. Why I kept running toward danger. Why chaos felt safer than stillness.

Now I know:

Trauma didn't just leave scars—it rewired my entire nervous system.

I wasn't broken.

I was *engineered* to survive. But that night...I didn't want to survive.

I wanted to break.

And I did.

Shattered into something unrecognizable.

But in that ruin, I found the thing I'd spent a lifetime searching for:

The strength to rise.

Not just crawl out—*rise*.

To break the curse I'd been handed like a family heirloom. To stare evil in the face and call it by name.

Not the kind of evil that storms through doors.

Not loud, not obvious.

But smooth.

Charming.

Calculating.

It wore the face of love.

It smiled with lies.

It called itself narcissism.

Looking back, I see why psychology gripped me. I wasn't just curious—I was *desperate*. Desperate to understand why I was the way I was. Why I hurt the way I did.

I played the victim because I didn't know how *not* to.

High-stress, high-risk situations felt like home. They mirrored my inner world—chaotic, unrelenting. And in that chaos, I felt strangely in control.

But I couldn't keep living like that. Not anymore.

I finally had the insight to know myself—And the obligation to *honor* that knowing.

Still, one thing gnawed at me: Why couldn't I visit my father's grave?

Jack drove the U-Haul. Daizy curled up in my lap, warm and breathing proof that I wasn't alone.

I flipped open the NLP workbook. A sentence jumped out and grabbed me by the throat: *"If you're not getting the result you want, change what you're doing. Take responsibility for the communication."*

I'd been waiting for my dad to come and find *me*.

To apologize.

To fix it.

But healing doesn't come with apologies.

It doesn't come from blame.

It comes when you decide to stop the bleeding.

I had to forgive him. But more than that—I had to forgive myself.

I thought about my childhood—how I pushed people away. Even the ones who tried to help.

It wasn't all my fault. But it wasn't all theirs, either.

I'd been fighting the hands that reached to hold me. But now I was the one reaching out—to myself.

As I packed up my life, leaving most of it behind, I wondered: Is this what my mother felt?

My grandmother? Shoving dreams and heartbreak into the trunk of a car and driving toward the unknown?

We try so damn hard not to become them. But they live in us. In blood.

In bone. In the way we love, and in the way we leave.

And maybe that's not a curse. Maybe that's the lesson.

We can't escape them.

But we can *evolve*.

We can forgive.

And we can finally—finally—own our part in the story.

Even though I was leaving behind family, friends, familiarity...I knew something I had never known before:

I was going to be okay.

Because for the first time—I believed I was *worthy*.

Worthy of love.

Worthy of peace.

Worthy of a life that belonged to me.

I wasn't wrong.

I was just different.

And for once... I didn't apologize for it.

The road ahead would break me open again. I knew that. But this time, I wouldn't shatter.

I had my dog. A full tank of gas. A name in Oregon. And a wildfire in my chest.

Not the kind that consumes. The kind that *refines*.

Not everything that burns is meant to be mourned. Some fires are for releasing. Some for rebirth.

This wasn't an escape. This was becoming.

A blank page.

A new chapter.

One I would *never* let anyone else write for me again.

Breathe, Chrissy.

You're not lost. You're arriving.

A stranger once told me: "The burdens we carry aren't meant to break us—they're meant to rip us open, to reveal our humanity. And in that rawness, we find our purpose: to share what we've learned. To become a light for others. So they know—they're not alone."

And neither are you.

Not now.

Not ever.

Burn the letters.

Forgive.

Release the chains.

Silence the Bad Witch whispering you're not enough.

Oh—and as for Frank?

Well...That's another story. One that deserves its own telling—with a cup of tea.

# Acknowledgments

This book almost never existed.

This book is made of pain. Of survival. Of silence finally broken.

**Michael Grossman**—thank you for being a quiet force in my corner. Your belief in my voice came when I didn't know I had one. You never asked for anything in return, only that I keep going. That kind of encouragement stays with a person. It stayed with me.

**Steven**, there are no words big enough. You were there through all of it: the breaking, the rebuilding, the hiding, the truth-telling. You never tried to fix me. You just held space. You supported this book emotionally, financially, spiritually—without hesitation. You were the one who told me to write when I thought I had nothing left to say. Thank you for loving me through all the versions of myself I had to become just to survive. You are my Hero.

**Mark Spencer**, my editor and witness to this entire evolution—God bless your patience. You read every messy draft. You didn't flinch when I ripped the story open again. And again. And again. You never complained—only encouraged. You pushed me to be a better writer and showed me how. This book would not exist without your fierce honesty and your kind belief. You didn't just edit the book—you held it like it mattered. And it did.

**Ms. G**, my 10th grade English teacher—thank you for seeing something in a lost, tired teenager that even I couldn't see. You were the first person who told me my words meant something. That belief carried me further than you'll ever know.

**My children** may this book help you understand why Mommy took so long to return to herself.

*Christine*

# What more...

To help you get the most out
of the book.

**DOWNLOAD
FREE GIFT**

- Pre-book reading prompts
- Chapter-by-chapter prompts
  - Pre-chapter prompts
  - Post-chapter prompts
- Post-book reading prompts
  Reflective prompts

## Chapter-by-Chapter e-Book

# Free e-Book

You deserve support. You deserve peace.

Dear Reader,
Thank you for reading Burnt Letters.
If this book resonated with you, I would be deeply grateful if you'd
consider leaving a short review. Even a few words can help this
story reach women who are still quietly asking, "Was it really that
bad?"

You can leave a review here:

Thank you for being here — and for
allowing this story to matter.

www.ingramcontent.com/pod-product-compliance
Lightning Source LLC
Chambersburg PA
CBHW020249130626
46549CB00005B/2140